Solid Foun  s

LIFE OF
MOSES

*Blueprints for 30 messages
built upon God's Word*

David Faust

STANDARD
PUBLISHING

Cincinnati, Ohio

Cover design by Grannan Graphic Design LTD

Interior design by Robert E. Korth

Edited by Jim Eichenberger
© 2000 by Standard Publishing
All rights reserved.
Printed in the U.S.A.

Solid Foundation™ is a trademark of
Standard Publishing, Cincinnati, Ohio.
A division of Standex International Corporation.
07 06 05 04 03 02 01 00   5 4 3 2 1

Contents

WILDERNESS WANDERING (SIXTEEN MESSAGES ON SPIRITUAL GROWTH BASED ON THE LIFE AND WRITINGS OF MOSES)

Prince of Egypt, Prophet of God

Hebrews 11:23-29

Did he look like Charlton Heston? I don't know. But I do know this: Other than Jesus himself, and perhaps the apostle Paul, it's likely that no other figure in all of history has exerted more influence on mankind than did Moses.

The first five books of the Bible are of his authorship. He held in his hands the original tablets of stone that bore the Ten Commandments. He was raised as a prince of Egypt, refined as a shepherd in Midian, and transformed into a prophet of God. Let us examine some elements of that remarkable life.

I. HIS FAITHFUL PARENTS SPARED HIS LIFE (v. 23).

A. "By faith Moses' parents hid him for three months" at the risk of their own lives, for Pharaoh had ordered that every Hebrew baby boy must be thrown into the river and drowned (Exodus 1:22).

B. "They saw he was no ordinary child." By faith, godly parents see the potential in their children and pray for the next generation to accomplish extraordinary things for the glory of God.

C. "They were not afraid of the king's edict." When parents bravely decide to "obey God rather than men" (see Acts 5:29), they model courage and commitment to their children. Years later Moses had to stand up against Pharaoh's stubborn, sinful will. It must have strengthened his resolve to review the story of his birth parents' faith.

II. HIS FAITHFUL DECISIONS SHAPED HIS LIFE (vv. 24-27).

A. Moses lived 120 years, and his life can be divided into three 40-year segments. The first 40 years he was a prince in Egypt. The second 40 years (after he killed an Egyptian who had mistreated a fellow Israelite) he was a fugitive and a shepherd in Midian. During the last 40 years, he led the Hebrews out of Egyptian bondage (Acts 7:23-34). Along the way, Moses made several significant decisions, each one guided by his faith in the Lord:

1. He decided who he would be: not "the son of Pharaoh's daughter," but a servant of God (v. 24).
2. He decided what group of people he would join, even though it meant being "mistreated along with the people of God" (v. 25a).
3. Taking the long view of life, he determined to act righteously and respon-

sibly "rather than to enjoy the pleasures of sin for a short time" (v. 25b).

4. He chose spiritual priorities over material ones, and "regarded disgrace for the sake of Christ as of greater value than the treasures of Egypt" (v. 26a).

5. He believed God's promises for the future and "was looking ahead to his reward" (v. 26b).

6. He persevered over the long haul because he was convinced of the reality of God and he "saw him who is invisible" (v. 27).

B. When we have difficult decisions to make, we need to follow Moses' example. Remember who we are and whose we are, look at the big picture, put God's kingdom first, keep our eyes on the goal, and stay faithful because we're confident God is real and he's leading our steps.

III. HIS FAITHFUL INFLUENCE HONORED HIS LORD (vv. 28, 29).

A. Moses' obedience to God was a matter of life and death—for himself and for many others. "He kept the Passover and the sprinkling of blood," which vividly portray the salvation ultimately accomplished by the sacrifice of Christ (v. 28).

B. Under his leadership more than half a million people experienced God's deliverance and protection as they walked safely through the parted waters of the Red Sea (v. 29).

ILLUSTRATIONS

Through the eyes of faith. If you had been standing by the Nile when Moses' mother placed her three-month-old son in a basket and left him there, would you have guessed that this tiny Hebrew boy would become one of history's best-known leaders? If you had stood near the manger where a young virgin named Mary had placed her baby wrapped in swaddling clothes, would you have realized this humble infant was the only-begotten Son of God? We don't always see the big picture, but God does. Through the eyes of faith, we see "him who is invisible" (Hebrews 11:27).

Hold on to something solid. Two men fell into the Niagara River. As they were being swept swiftly toward the falls and certain death, someone on shore saw their plight, tied a rope to a tree trunk, and tossed the rope into the water. Both men gratefully grabbed onto the rope and tried to hang on. Soon, however, a log floating in the water bumped into one of the men. Feeling the large log and instinctively sensing that something that big must be more secure than a flimsy rope, the man released his grip on the rope and grabbed onto the log. Soon, however, both he and the log were swept over the falls, while the man who hung onto the rope was rescued—because however flimsy it might have felt, the rope was tied to something solid on the shore. When we're drowning in sin and despair, we may find it tempting to let go of our faith and grab onto man-made philosophies that seem strong and secure. But our only real security is in the Lord and his truth. Don't ever let go of your faith in him (Colossians 2:6-8).

The Reluctant Leader:
Serving God in Spite of Your Weaknesses
Exodus 3 & 4

The demands of ministry sometimes seem overwhelming. But if you ever feel reluctant to serve God, you're in good company. Jeremiah greeted God's call to service with two excuses: "I'm too young" and "I'm not a capable speaker" (Jeremiah 1:6). The apostle Paul pondered the weighty responsibilities of ministry and wondered, "Who is equal to such a task?" (2 Corinthians 2:16). Moses was one of the greatest leaders of all time, but his immediate response to God was reluctance rather than confidence.

I. A SURPRISING CALL (3:1-10)

A. It's surprising that a prince of Egypt would find himself in such lowly circumstances, tending sheep in the desert of Midian (v. 1). (Before we're ready for our most significant work, sometimes God waits until we've learned the lessons of humility and brokenness.)

B. It's surprising that the Lord used a burning bush to get Moses' attention (vv. 2-5).
1. Bushes were commonplace; a burning bush would be unusual but not necessarily miraculous. This bush, however, continued burning without burning up—a bright, miraculous illustration of the inextinguishable power and glory of God.
2. God didn't speak to Moses in an elaborate sanctuary or an ornate temple, but amid the rugged wilderness surroundings of Moses' daily work as a shepherd. If we're attuned to God's presence, even our commonplace surroundings become holy ground.

C. It's surprising what the Lord wanted Moses to do (vv. 6-10):
1. Lead the Israelites from a land of slavery to a land of prosperity.
2. Confront powerful Pharaoh when Moses himself was a fugitive who years before had left Egypt in fear.

II. A HESITANT RESPONSE (3:11–4:13)

A. Moses offered five basic excuses (paraphrased below) to explain why he didn't feel qualified to be God's designated leader. God countered each excuse with a word of assurance.
1. **Moses:** "Who am I to do this?"

God: "I will be with you." What matters most is not who Moses is, but who God is (3:11, 12).
2. **Moses:** "What if people ask me your name?"
   God: "Tell them, 'I am who I am.' I've always existed and always will." The eternal God could foresee the outcome of all this (3:13-22).
3. **Moses:** "O.K., but what if they don't?"
   God: "I'll give you some signs of my miraculous power" (4:1-9).
4. **Moses:** "But Lord, how can I lead when I've never been a very good public speaker? (And I haven't gotten any better during this conversation!)."
   God: "I made your mouth! If I call you, I'll also equip you" (4:10, 11).
5. **Moses:** "I'd still prefer you send somebody else."
   God: "You're trying my patience, Moses! Your brother Aaron is a good speaker. His strengths will fill the gaps where you are weak. Now quit making excuses and get to work!" (4:14-17).

B. When Moses and Aaron obeyed the Lord's call, God kept his promises (4:29-31).

III. A CONTEMPORARY APPLICATION
A. When God calls us . . .
1. He will give us jobs that fit our abilities. "Each one should use whatever gift he has received to serve others" (1 Peter 4:10).
2. He will enable us with strength beyond our own. He "is able to do immeasurably more than all we ask or imagine" (Ephesians 3:20).
3. He will use us in spite of our weaknesses. "Our competence comes from God" (2 Corinthians 3:5).

B. When God calls us to serve, we must . . .
1. Be honest about our objections, but willing to follow his instructions.
2. Allow God's grace-givings to overcome our misgivings.
3. Know that there's more at stake than our personal happiness. "Anyone who does not carry his cross and follow me cannot be my disciple" (Luke 14:27).
4. Use what we already have in our hands (Exodus 4:2) instead of griping about what we don't have.

ILLUSTRATIONS
Excuses, excuses. Excuses are common. "Sorry, Preacher, I can't help because I'm going to do some homework on my computer." "Sorry I can't turn in my homework, Professor, but my computer crashed." "Mom, I didn't do the laundry because I had homework to do." Nobody has heard more excuses than the Lord has. But when it comes to believing in God, we're all "without excuse" (Romans 1:20).

What is that in your hand? At a leprosy hospital in Addis Ababa, Ethiopia, I saw a young woman who had lost both her hands to the disease. She was weaving a beautiful tablecloth—with her feet. If she could do that with no hands, what am I doing with the two hands I have?

The Obedient Leader:
Choosing to Do Right

Exodus 6:28–7:24

Obedience isn't a very popular concept today. I doubt that anytime soon *Time* magazine will feature a photo of their "person of the year" with a caption that says, "He Just Obeyed God." In today's culture, it is more popular to resist authority than to obey it, flaunting self-will rather than complying with God's will.

But it's still true that, as the hymnwriter put it, "There's no other way to be happy in Jesus, but to trust and obey." Moses demonstrated that a godly leader follows God and chooses to do right even when it's hard to obey.

I. OBEDIENT LEADERS RECOGNIZE WHO IS IN CHARGE (6:28, 29).

A. God left no doubt about his sovereignty. He told Moses, "I am the Lord." Have you really settled in your mind the fact that God is in charge? Before you can lead others to obey God, you must obey him yourself. Have you surrendered your will, your schedule, your priorities, your money, your attitudes, your goals, and your relationships to God?

B. When we recognize God is in charge, we respond humbly as Jesus did in the Garden of Gethsemane ("not as I will, but as you will"—Matthew 26:39), and as Peter did on the shores of Galilee ("Because you say so, I will let down the nets"—Luke 5:5). If we respect the Lordship of Christ, and his will is clear, we should respond by simply saying, "Because you say so, I will obey."

II. OBEDIENT LEADERS UNDERSTAND THEIR MISSION (6:29).

A. Moses' job was to tell Pharaoh (a resistant audience) everything (a comprehensive message) God had told him (an unpopular message).

B. God doesn't speak to us in exactly the same way he spoke to Moses and the other prophets, but he does speak to us directly and clearly through his Word. It's our mission to communicate the gospel faithfully, proclaiming "the whole will of God" (Acts 20:27).

III. OBEDIENT LEADERS ACCEPT GOD'S HELP (6:30–7:5).

A. *Moses was weak, but God could use him anyway.* Constantly aware of his own weaknesses, Moses repeated the same excuse he had offered earlier at the burning bush: "I speak with faltering lips, why would Pharaoh listen to me?" (6:30, compare 4:10).

B. *Moses couldn't do it all himself, but God provided a partner who was strong where Moses was weak.* His brother Aaron became his spokesman (7:1, 2). Sometimes leaders disobey God by trying to do everything ourselves instead of working in harmony with others God has put around us to make up for our weaknesses.

C. *Moses was merely a man, but God provided power to do things Moses could never accomplish on his own.* God's Word was powerfully expressed through Moses' ministry (7:2). The 10 plagues were a tool of judgment and revelation (7:3-5). Moses' staff became the staff of God (7:8-13). What do you hold in your hand? What can the Lord do through you that you couldn't accomplish on your own?

IV. OBEDIENT LEADERS DO THINGS GOD'S WAY NO MATTER WHAT (7:6).

A. Moses and Aaron "did just as the Lord commanded them" (7:6). They may not have understood the Lord's plan completely. They were old enough (80 and 83) to have been a bit set in their ways (7:7). But they obeyed.

B. What is the Lord asking you to do? Will you simply trust and obey?

ILLUSTRATIONS

Lighthouses. In Prince Edward Island, Canada, quaint-looking white lighthouses dot the countryside near the sea. To the eyes of a tourist, these picturesque structures are mere curiosities. But to the eyes of a sailor, they provide practical guidance and direction for navigation. To some people, the Bible is merely a curiosity—a quaint, nostalgic token of a long-forgotten age. But to the Christian, God's Word is a light in the darkness and a lamp that helps us find our way. We cannot navigate today's rough cultural waters without the guidance of Scripture.

Spreading our wings. In New Zealand, beautiful white birds called gannets gather on the white stone cliffs overlooking the sea. These graceful creatures can fly with minimal flapping of their wings. At times they almost appear to simply step off the cliffs, spread their wings, and soar as they catch the drafts of wind currents that lift them up. God wants us to step out in faith. If we do, he will lift us up and carry us where he wants us to go.

The Resilient Leader:
Persevering in Spite of Criticism
Exodus 14:10-15

Anyone who attempts something worthwhile for the Lord will endure criticism. Jesus endured repeated verbal barbs from his critics, and said, "If they persecuted me, they will persecute you also" (John 15:20). The apostle Paul was the target of insults (1 Thessalonians 2:2), and Peter wrote to encourage Christians who were facing malicious slander (1 Peter 2:12; 3:16; 4:14). Few leaders ever faced more criticism than Moses. His example has a lot to teach us about criticism and how to respond to it.

I. UNDERSTANDING CRITICISM

A. Critics sometimes express legitimate concern. As the Israelites fled from Egypt, they saw Pharaoh's army in hot pursuit (v. 10). The danger was real. Not every criticism is mean-spirited, and not every critic is badly-intentioned. Sometimes our critics are our best friends, for their warnings can prevent us from making serious mistakes. "Listen to advice and accept instruction, and in the end you will be wise" (Proverbs 19:20).

B. Critics often are motivated by fear. The Israelites "were terrified" (v. 10b). People lash out at others when they feel threatened or endangered. It's hard to blame the Israelites for feeling afraid when the Egyptians were threatening to cut them down. Wise leaders identify their followers' fears and take them seriously.

C. Critics frequently look for a leader to blame. Leaders are lightning rods for criticism. In fact, absorbing the frustration followers express when problems arise may be a legitimate role for a leader. In vv. 11 and 12, the Israelites immediately turned to Moses with sarcasm ("Were [there] no graves in Egypt?"), personal accusations ("What have you done to us?"), "I-told-you-sos" ("Didn't we say to you in Egypt, 'Leave us alone . . . ?'"), and questionable logic ("It would have been better for us to serve the Egyptians").

D. Critics often are motivated by envy. Power plays and selfish ambition are nothing new. Moses' own sister and brother, Miriam and Aaron, eventually spoke against him saying, "Hasn't [God] also spoken through us?" (Numbers 12:1, 2). Likewise, Jesus' disciples frequently argued among themselves about who was the greatest (Luke 9:46; 22:24).

E. Unchecked and unresolved, criticism will poison morale. During the Israelites' 40 years in the wilderness, Moses endured relentless criticism and rebellious attitudes from his followers (Exodus 16:1-3; 17:1-4; Numbers 11:1-10; 12:1, 2; 14:1-12; 16:1-3; 20:1-5). It's a tribute to God's faithfulness and Moses' resilience that he was able to persevere. It's hard for leaders to do their best work when critics are constantly hounding them.

II. RESPONDING TO CRITICISM

A. When you're wrong, admit it—and learn from your critics. "The way of a fool seems right to him, but a wise man listens to advice" (Proverbs 12:15).

B. When you're right, stand firm—and learn from your critics. Even a misguided criticism can contain some truth. Even a critic who misunderstands you can help you see flaws in the way you're communicating an idea.

C. When you're afraid, trust God. Leaders experience fear just as much as their followers do. But a true leader will always point people to God and his strength. That's what Moses did (v. 13).

D. When more talk won't help, be still. Sometimes leaders (and followers) are tempted to talk about every angle of an issue until there's nothing left to say. When words can't resolve a pressing problem, it's good to follow the advice of Moses: "The Lord will fight for you; you need only to be still" (v. 14).

E. Once God's direction is clear, move on. The worst response is to allow negative criticism to immobilize God's people. God told Moses, "Tell the Israelites to move on" (v. 15). If God has a purpose to fulfill, he will provide the resources and strength to accomplish it—even against impossible odds (vv. 15-31).

ILLUSTRATIONS

Tearing down. When I was a teenager, I worked for a carpenter. One day, he gave me an ax and a crowbar, and asked me to take down part of an old building. In a short time I accomplished the task. Building a new house took a lot longer—and it took a lot more skill. My boss, a master carpenter, planned and measured, cut and nailed. Working together over time, we built something strong and lasting. Anyone can tear something down. It takes patient, united effort to build something up.

Different kinds of critics. According to Dr. Mike Shannon, who preaches at First Christian Church, Johnson City, Tennessee, there are four main types of critics in the church: (1) the chronic complainer, who finds something wrong with almost everything, (2) the traditionalist, who resists change, (3) the impatient visionary, who wants immediate change, and (4) the power-hungry manipulator, who wants to be in charge. With so many critics around, surely one of the most frequently violated commands of Scripture is Philippians 2:14: "Do everything without complaining or arguing."

The Cooperative Leader: Accepting Help From Others

Exodus 18:5-27

Are you a team player? Are you willing to accept advice and help from others? While leaders need courage to stand alone, we need support and encouragement from others as well (Ecclesiastes 4:9-12). Teamwork models unity, fills gaps created by our personal weaknesses, and gives us a chance to practice patience and love as we work together with others who are as imperfect as we are.

Even Jesus surrounded himself with a group of men who worked with him side by side. The apostle Paul shared his ministry with trusted coworkers like Barnabas, Silas, Timothy, and Titus. While Moses was a strong leader who stood tall on his own, he also worked side by side with his brother Aaron, his sister Miriam, and military leaders like Joshua and Caleb. On one occasion, he also heeded some wise advice from his father-in-law, a priest named Reuel (better known as Jethro).

I. A HEALTHY RELATIONSHIP (vv. 5-7)

A. *Respect.* Jethro courteously sent word ahead to inform Moses of his coming visit (v. 6). When he arrived, Moses bowed before his father-in-law (some fathers-in-law would think this is great!) and kissed him (a token of great respect in Middle Eastern cultures). "They greeted each other," cordially, it appears (v. 7).

B. *Communication.* "Moses told his father-in-law about everything" that had been happening, both good and bad, since they last were together (v. 8).

C. *Encouragement.* "Jethro was delighted" with the news Moses reported to him, and he encouraged Moses' faith that God was with him (vv. 9-12).

II. SOME OVERWHELMING PROBLEMS (vv. 13-18)

A. Moses had good intentions. He cared about God's people. He was willing to work long hours. He took seriously his responsibility to lead the people and show them God's will.

B. Yet what Moses was doing was "not good" (v. 17). He was on a path toward burnout. No doubt the people were growing frustrated by the long waits outside of Moses' "courtroom." Other leaders were being deprived of an opportunity to develop and exercise their own gifts. And Moses was spending precious time on minor matters that others could have handled.

III. SOME GOOD ADVICE (vv. 19-23)

A. Jethro's advice to Moses? Give the right kind of work to the right kind of men within the right kind of organization.

1. The right kind of work: Moses should retain his role as the primary prophet and teacher, while other matters could be handled by . . .
2. The right kind of men: capable, God-fearing, trustworthy, not interested in gaining money or power dishonestly. These men could serve effectively if they were part of . . .
3. The right kind of organization: ranging from small groups of ten (where leaders with less experience or skill could develop their abilities) to large groups of thousands (where the finest of leaders could find themselves challenged and fulfilled), with midsized groups of fifties and hundreds as well.

B. When a similar problem arose in the early church, the apostles followed a similar strategy: find some other godly men and delegate some of the responsibility to them (Acts 6:1-7).

IV. A POSITIVE RESULT (vv. 24-27)

A. Moses showed humility and integrity as a leader because he was willing to accept and implement his father-in-law's wise recommendation.

B. Wouldn't God's work move forward more smoothly . . . If we listened to wise, godly advice? ("Plans fail for lack of counsel, but with many advisers they succeed," Proverbs 15:22.) . . . If every member of God's family did his or her share of the work? . . . If we quit trying to do everything ourselves? May God give us cooperative leaders, willing to work together as a team for the good of God's kingdom!

ILLUSTRATIONS

Overspending. You can't spend $500 per week if you're only making $300 per week at your job. Eventually, overspending will catch up with you. In the same way, each of us has a certain amount of time and physical energy to invest—even in good causes like the Lord's work. We need to be good stewards of our time and energy lest we grow weary in well-doing and needlessly burn out.

Too close to see. If you move a page of your Bible or church bulletin closer and closer to your eyes, eventually it will come so close that the words begin to blur. Likewise, sometimes the closer you are to a situation, the harder it is to see things clearly. That's why we need respected, trustworthy Christian friends to hold us accountable and point out those areas of weakness and need that we struggle to see on our own.

The Courageous Leader:
Daring to Confront Sin
Exodus 32:1-35

One of the hardest parts of leadership is confronting and dealing with sin in our own lives and in the lives of those we lead. It is especially tough in today's culture, where we're urged to be tolerant and nonjudgmental even toward actions and beliefs past generations would have quickly labeled as wrong. People often ask, "What gives you the right to tell anyone else what to do?"

God's leaders must lead with gentleness and love. We must examine ourselves honestly, and humbly recognize our own weaknesses before attempting to correct someone else (Matthew 7:1-5; Galatians 6:1). But God also calls us to "correct, rebuke and encourage—with great patience and careful instruction" (2 Timothy 4:2). This requires a combination of discernment and tact, wisdom and courage.

Long ago, Moses had to deal with a deeply disappointing and terribly destructive sin among the Hebrew people. It happened right on the heels of the great mountaintop experience when Moses received the Law from God on Mt. Sinai. Exodus 32 tells how the people fell into sin while Moses was gone. What can we learn from this incident?

I. RECOGNIZING SIN FOR WHAT IT IS

A. "The sins of some men are obvious" (1 Timothy 5:24), but others are more subtle. In every case, sin is harmful. Like a roaring lion, the devil prowls about "looking for someone to devour" (1 Peter 5:8). Leaders must be on guard, helping those entrusted to our care to resist the devil. Sometimes our love for people makes us overlook their sin or take it lightly. But in reality, our love for people should make us want God's best for them, which means dealing honestly with sinful attitudes or behaviors so the door can be opened to repentance, forgiveness, and reconciliation.

B. Notice six facts about the sin Moses had to confront:
1. *It sprang from impatience (v. 1).* The people thought Moses was taking too long to come down from the mountain.
2. *It brought down a great man (vv. 2-6).* Aaron—Moses' own older brother —became a ringleader in this sin. Shouldn't Aaron have known better than to get involved in idolatry? Why was he so weak? Why did he play to the crowd instead of advising them to wait patiently for Moses' return? Even great men are susceptible to temptation.
3. *It displeased the Lord (vv. 7-10).* What an insult! God's people worshiped their own creation—a calf that was nothing but yesterday's earrings!

4. *It cheapened what should have been a great moment (vv. 15-20)*. Moses was coming down the mountain with stone tablets in his hands that were "the work of God" (v. 16). This should have been a moment of joy. But instead, Moses became angry when he saw the people breaking the very Commandments God had engraved on the tablets.
5. *It led to lame excuses (vv. 21-24)*. Aaron tried to blame others ("Boys will be boys, Moses!") and act as if the golden calf "just happened" ("I threw [the gold] into the fire, and out came this calf").
6. *It led to deadly consequences (vv. 25-29)*. This punishment seems terribly harsh, and we can be glad God deals with us more patiently today under the new covenant of grace. (Here, 3,000 lawbreakers were slain. On Pentecost, 3,000 lawbreakers were forgiven.) But the things that happened to the ancient Hebrews "occurred as examples, to keep us from setting our hearts on evil things as they did" (1 Corinthians 10:6). Idolatry was a cancer that had to be eradicated to save the Israelite nation as a whole. Spiritually speaking, sin still leads to tragic consequences. "The wages of sin is death" (Romans 6:23).

II. RESPONDING TO SIN REDEMPTIVELY

A. Moses courageously confronted the sin of his people. He bluntly told them, "You have committed a great sin" (v. 30). We must dare to speak the truth and hold one another accountable to do God's will (Matthew 18:15-17).

B. Moses prayed to the Lord in behalf of his people (vv. 31, 32). He loved the people so much, he even suggested that his own name be blotted out of God's book lest any of them be lost. God didn't accept this suggestion. But centuries later, God sent his own Son to bear the consequences for our sin (Romans 5:8-10). Earnestly, lovingly, boldly, we must call our friends and neighbors back to the God who loves them. "Whoever turns a sinner from the error of his way will save him from death and cover over a multitude of sins" (James 5:20).

ILLUSTRATIONS

Misplaced "I." Some of the most frequently misspelled words in the English language are words like *relief, belief, receive, siege, seize,* and *weird,* because people tend to put the "I" in the wrong place. Likewise, some of our most common spiritual mistakes occur because we put the "I" in the wrong place. Selfishly, we focus on "what I want" instead of "what God wants."

Deadly leadership. In 1982, a special stunt team composed of four Air Force pilots routinely flew their planes in such tight formations that the first plane led the way and the other pilots couldn't see where they were going. They were trained simply to follow their leader and go wherever he led them. Tragically, the pilot of the lead plane went badly off course, and the three others followed him right into the ground and were killed. God wants us to follow wise, biblical leadership; but to avoid spiritual disaster, we must make sure the leaders we follow are taking us in the right direction.

The Worshiping Leader:
Seeking God's Presence Above All Else
Exodus 33:12–34:8

Did you ever meet a famous person? The most important person we'll ever meet is the Lord God himself, who invites us to come boldly into his presence. He alone is worthy of our highest praise, worship, and honor.

Immediately after leading the Israelites through the divided waters of the Red Sea, Moses led the people in a song of praise to the Lord (Exodus 15:1-18). As God continued to reveal himself to Moses, eventually Moses knew the Lord so well, the Lord would speak to him "face to face, as a man speaks with his friend" (Exodus 33:11). What can we learn about worship from this great man of God?

I. THE PRIORITY OF PRAISE (33:12, 13)

A. *Before you can lead others to know the Lord, first you must know him yourself.* This is a basic principle, but it's easy to overlook. Moses' prayer was not simply, "Teach me your ways so I'll have something to say when I stand up to teach and preach." His prayer was, "Teach me your ways so I may know you" (33:13).

B. It's tempting for Christians—and especially church leaders—to become so busy serving God we take no time to praise him. But there's no substitute for simply knowing God. What matters most is not what others see, but what God sees. It's not what happens "up front" that counts; it's what happens "deep down" as our hearts praise and honor our Creator and Lord.

C. That's why praise was such a priority for Jesus (Matthew 11:25), for the early church (Acts 2:47), for the apostle Paul (Ephesians 1:3), and for the apostle Peter (1 Peter 1:3). Praising God must take first priority.

II. THE PRESENCE OF GOD (33:14-16)

A. *Before you can lead others where the Lord wants them to go, first you must know that the Lord is with you wherever YOU go.* The Lord assured Moses, "My Presence will go with you, and I will give you rest" (33:14). Moses responded, "If your Presence does not go with us, do not send us up from here" (33:15).

B. The principle is simple: No Presence, no power. How difficult it is when we try to serve the Lord while we have no sense of his abiding presence and strength.

C. Graciously, the Lord Jesus promised his neverending presence with his disciples (Matthew 28:20). They responded by continuing in praise (Luke 24:50-53).

III. THE FOCUS OF PRAISE (33:17–34:8)

A. *Before you can do the Lord's work, first you need to know his character.* Moses' request to God: "Now show me your glory" (33:18). God responded by making it clear there is far more to God than Moses could comprehend (33:19-23).

B. Yet Moses would indeed receive a powerful glimpse of God's glory if he would approach God . . .

1. With obedience. He had to follow specific commands: chisel out two stone tablets (to replace the ones Moses earlier had broken in anger—32:19), be ready in the morning, come up onto Mt. Sinai alone (34:1-4).
2. With reverence. He "bowed to the ground at once" (34:8).

C. Thanks to Jesus Christ, we can approach God's throne of grace with confidence and joy (Hebrews 4:16; 10:19-25; 12:28). Yet, like Moses, we need to approach God with an attitude of reverent obedience. It's good to "be ready in the morning" (34:2)—by starting each day with personal devotions and worship. Times of private prayer equip us to perform public ministry.

IV. THE PRODUCT OF PRAISE

A. *Before you face a world filled with change, you need to worship the One who never changes.* The Lord who showed himself to Moses is still the same God today. He never changes (Malachi 3:6). He is still compassionate, gracious, slow to anger, abounding in love and faithfulness, and he still possesses all the other praiseworthy qualities he revealed to Moses (34:5-7).

B. Moses' time of worship left him empowered, emboldened, and radiant (34:29-35). What will happen if you and I spend more time praising our wonderful Lord?

ILLUSTRATION

Groping in the dark. The other evening my wife, Candy, had gone shopping and my son and I were home when a thunderstorm blew through our neighborhood and knocked out the power. My son and I weren't worried; we had plenty of candles in the house. Unfortunately, though, we couldn't find any matches, for Candy had moved them from their familiar drawer to a different location. And when I grabbed our only flashlight, I discovered that the batteries were dead. So until Candy returned home, Matt and I groped in the dark, unable to see or do anything but wait. Did you ever find yourself groping in the dark in a spiritual sense? Aren't you glad God has made himself known? That's why "you may declare the praises of him who called you out of darkness into his wonderful light" (1 Peter 2:9).

The Imperfect Leader:
Serving God Faithfully in Spite of Your Failures
Numbers 20:1-13

Abraham, the great man of faith, lied and told people his wife, Sarah, was his sister. David overcame Goliath but succumbed to his lust for Bathsheba. Peter boasted that he would never disown Jesus even at the cost of his own death, yet three times he denied the Lord and later wept over his failure. Likewise, Moses was a great leader, but he was imperfect. Numbers chapter 20 describes a serious and costly mistake he made. In this account we see important lessons about self-control.

I. MOSES' PATIENCE HAD WORN THIN.

A. His sister, Miriam, died (v. 1). This must have been hard on Moses. Miriam was his older sister, the one who had watched him as an infant when his mother placed him in a basket and put him among the reeds of the Nile River. Miriam was the one who had suggested to Pharaoh's daughter that Moses' birth mother should be his nurse (Exodus 2:1-10). She had joined Moses in songs of praise when the Israelites escaped from Egypt (Exodus 15:19-21). Even when she and her brother Aaron spoke out against his leadership, Moses prayed for Miriam (Numbers 12:1-15). It must have saddened him greatly to bury his sister there in the Desert of Zin. It's hard to be at your best when you're experiencing grief.

B. The people had no water (v. 2a). It's hard to be upbeat when you're hot, tired, and thirsty—and responsible for a large group of people who are growing increasingly critical.

C. The people had a bad attitude (vv. 2b-5). The people rebelled against Moses' leadership. They wallowed in self-pity, and even griped that they'd have been better off to have died earlier in the journey. They saw nothing good in their current circumstances. It's hard to be at your best when you're hit by wave after wave of discouragement.

II. MOSES KNEW HOW HE *SHOULD* RESPOND.

A. He immediately took his concerns to the Lord (v. 6). That's how we should respond, too. After all, God "daily bears our burdens" (Psalm 68:19) and says, "Cast all your anxiety on him because he cares for you" (1 Peter 5:7).

B. He listened to God's instructions (vv. 7, 8). The Lord gave Moses clear, detailed, step-by-step instructions about how to deal with the situation. Likewise, God has told us in his Word how to deal with difficult circumstances. But like the apostle Paul, often our problem is that, even though we know the good we ought to do, we don't do it (Romans 7:14-20). We're imperfect, not because God hasn't told us the right thing to do, but because we lack the willpower and self-control to do what we know is right.

III. MOSES' ANGER MADE HIM DO SOMETHING FOOLISH.

A. He followed some of God's instructions, but not all (vv. 9-11). Evidently he lost his temper, and struck the rock with his staff—not once, but twice. While anger isn't necessarily evil (even God expresses righteous indignation), many foolish decisions are made and foolish words said when we've lost our temper. That's why Scripture warns, "In your anger do not sin" (Ephesians 4:26).

B. God's response to Moses' actions may seem rather harsh (v. 12). But when it comes to obeying God, a leader like Moses should be an example, not an exception. God made it clear that the lawgiver wasn't above the law.

IV. MOSES PAID A PRICE FOR HIS DISOBEDIENCE—YET GOD STILL SHOWED HIM GRACE.

A. Because of Moses' mistake, he wasn't allowed to enter the long-awaited promised land. A leader's mistakes can bring about costly consequences. That's why it's such a serious matter to accept the responsibilities of leadership in the first place. (See James 3:1.)

B. But in his grace, God still used Moses' imperfect act to resolve Israel's water crisis as water gushed out from the rock (v. 11). God can bless his people in spite of their leaders' mistakes. He still used Abraham's faith, David's devotion, and Peter's courage, even though these men had their faults. If we're willing, he can still use us—in spite of our imperfections. He wants us to come to him just as we are, sins and all, and let him mold us into the kind of servants he wants us to be.

ILLUSTRATION

Wild winds. On April 9, 1999, a powerful tornado tore through the northeast section of Cincinnati, Ohio. In just a few minutes' time, it destroyed 90 houses, tore roofs off many other homes and buildings, and leveled hundreds of trees. It doesn't take long for a storm to cause extensive damage. Likewise, a burst of uncontrolled anger can destroy relationships, ruin reputations, and diminish a person's credibility. James 1:19 is right: "Everyone should be quick to listen, slow to speak and slow to become angry."

The Faithful Leader:
Passing the Baton to the Next Generation
Deuteronomy 30:11-20; 31:1-8

A leader's job isn't finished until he passes on the mantle of leadership to others who will carry on God's work in the next generation. The apostle Paul wrote, "And the things you have heard me say in the presence of many witnesses entrust to reliable men who will also be qualified to teach others" (2 Timothy 2:2). Before Moses died, he reminded the people to be faithful to God, then he appointed and encouraged his successor, Joshua. The book of Deuteronomy (which means "second law" or "repetition of the law") tells how Moses repeated many of the laws God had given the people earlier. Moses warned and blessed the people and prepared them for his coming death. His greatest concern was for the people to remain faithful to the Lord in succeeding generations.

I. MOSES REMINDED THE PEOPLE TO BE FAITHFUL (30:11-20).
A. Obedience is difficult, but not impossible (30:11-14).

B. Obedience is ultimately a matter of life and death (30:15-18).

C. Obedience leads to incredible blessings (30:19, 20).

II. MOSES RECOGNIZED HIS OWN LIMITATIONS (31:1-6).
A. His mortality—"I am now a hundred and twenty years old" (31:1, 2a).

B. His inability to lead any farther—"I am no longer able to lead you" (31:2b).

C. The limitations of his life and service—"The Lord has said to me, 'You shall not cross the Jordan'" (31:2c).

D. The Lord's ability to lead the people on—"The Lord your God himself will cross over ahead of you" (31:3-5).

III. MOSES RECOGNIZED AND ENCOURAGED HIS SUCCESSOR (31:7, 8).
A. He affirmed the calling and giftedness of God's new man—"Then Moses summoned Joshua" (31:7a).

B. He affirmed Joshua publically—"in the presence of all Israel" (31:7b).

C. He encouraged Joshua verbally—"be strong and courageous" (31:7c).

D. He helped Joshua see clearly what his task would involve—"you must go with this people into the land . . . and you must divide it among them as their inheritance" (31:7d).

E. He reassured Joshua that God's presence and power would be with him— "he will never leave you nor forsake you" (31:8a).

F. He urged Joshua not to yield to fear or discouragement—"Do not be afraid; do not be discouraged" (31:8b).

ILLUSTRATIONS

Training your own replacement. Instead of encouraging an unhealthy overdependence on our own skills and personalities, God's leaders need to prepare ourselves and our people for the time when we will no longer be present. The work must go on, even when we are gone. Every Paul needs to train a Timothy or two. Every Sunday school teacher needs an assistant, every small group leader an apprentice, every worship leader someone to train. Elders need to mentor young men to develop their leadership skills. Preachers need to groom and equip others to use their gifts to the fullest. It's a team effort. God's work is too important to let it be hindered by our egos, our desire to have our own way, or our desire for recognition. Train your own replacement, then rejoice in his or her accomplishments!

Smooth transitions. In football, it's important not to fumble the handoff. In track, it's important for relay racers not to drop the baton. In music, listeners appreciate a smooth transition from one passage of music to another. Likewise in the church, we need to do our best to make smooth transitions from one stage of the church's life to the next.

Godly Priorities:
Honor God by Putting Him First
Exodus 20:1-6

In college sports, teams compete for the honor of being listed among the nation's top ten schools. Television comedians make people laugh with funny top ten lists. But there's another top ten list that surpasses them all, and it's been around for more than 3,000 years.

By themselves, the Ten Commandments are not a plan of salvation. The closer we look at them, the more we realize how far we fall short and how much we need God's mercy. "Through the law we become conscious of sin" (Romans 3:20). These laws show us our need for the Savior, Jesus Christ. But at the same time, they challenge us to holy living by offering clear, memorable, unchanging standards of right and wrong. They remind us that character counts, and they describe for us several marks of a person of integrity. In this series of five messages, we'll look at two commandments each week and examine five steps to a more godly lifestyle. The first two Commandments deal with our priorities: putting God first in our lives.

I. WORSHIP THE RIGHT GOD.

A. God deserves our honor because of who he is. "I am the Lord your God" (vv. 1, 2a). He is the everlasting Father, the almighty, all-knowing, ever-present Lord.

B. God deserves our honor because of what he has done. "Who brought you out of Egypt, out of the land of slavery" (v. 2b). He is our creator, the author of life, the giver of hope, the redeemer and liberator of those in bondage.

C. God has no worthy rivals. "You shall have no other gods before me" (v. 3). Counterfeit money may look like the real thing, but it's worthless. A silk flower may look like the real thing, but it has no fragrance. Likewise, there is no substitute for the real God. Ancient people worshiped the sun, the moon, and fire. They had gods of fertility, of war, of love. First-century Athens even contained an altar to the unknown god (Acts 17:23). Modern people have found other substitutes: money, work, education, sports, friendships, man-made religions. But no one can take the place of God.

II. WORSHIP THE RIGHT GOD THE RIGHT WAY.

A. The second Commandment emphasizes our need to worship God in a way that pleases him. "You shall not make for yourself an idol," God says (v. 4).

This doesn't forbid making works of art. Even in Old Testament times, God gave men and women artistic skills with wood, cloth, and precious metals to be used for his glory—for example, in the construction of the tabernacle and later of the temple (Exodus 35:25–36:38; 1 Kings 7:13-51). However, this Commandment does forbid turning anything our hands have made into an object of worship.

B. Idolatry distorts our image of God. It diminishes the glory he deserves. It reverses the proper creation order by putting created things in the Creator's place (Romans 1:21-25).

C. God is passionately concerned about his relationship with us. He is "a jealous God" (v. 5)—not envious, petty, self-centered, or smothering, but a God who cares deeply for his people. False worship and other sins ruin families and bring harm to our children and grandchildren (v. 5), but God's desire is to bless "a thousand generations" to come (v. 6).

D. To worship God the right way, we need to worship "in spirit and in truth" (John 4:24). Our focus shouldn't be on buildings, pews, preachers, and programs, but on God. The right priorities put God, his kingdom, and his righteousness first (Matthew 6:33). Then all of life becomes a "worship service" so that whatever we do, we "do it all for the glory of God" (1 Corinthians 10:31).

ILLUSTRATIONS

Incidental religious content. My wife and I attended a holiday concert at our daughter's high school. The choir and orchestra performed traditional selections like "Joy to the World" and concluded with Handel's "Hallelujah Chorus." It was powerful music, but our enjoyment deflated a bit when we read the disclaimer someone had printed at the bottom of the program. It said, "This presentation of traditional holiday music includes incidental religious content. This content does not constitute an endorsement by the school district of any religion or religious doctrine." I understand that school officials feel pressured not to violate the separation of church and state. But it seemed sad to see magnificent lyrics dismissed as "incidental religious content"—as if to say, "Don't worry, none of us are taking these words too seriously. We don't really mean what we're singing." Sadder still, some church bulletins almost could include the same disclaimer! Do we simply go through the motions and mouth bland words, or do we worship God with our whole hearts?

Right worship. Augustine said, "Idolatry is worshiping anything that ought to be used, and using anything that ought to be worshiped."

Godly Lifestyle: Honor God With Your Speech and Your Schedule

Exodus 20:7-11

The Bible says, "Like a city whose walls are broken down is a man who lacks self-control" (Proverbs 25:28). Baseball legend Casey Stengel once said of Billy Martin, the flamboyant manager of the New York Yankees, "He can manage everyone but himself."

Do we manage our lives in a way that honors God? Do we exercise self-control in the way we use our tongues and schedule our time? To be people of integrity and develop character qualities that honor our Lord, we need to follow two more principles found in the Ten Commandments. We need to honor God with the way we speak, and with the way we spend our time.

I. SPEECH THAT SHOWS REVERENCE: RESPECT FOR GOD'S NAME

A. "You shall not misuse the name of the Lord your God" (v. 7). God's name is majestic (Psalm 8:1) and holy (Psalm 111:9; Matthew 6:9). To take his name "in vain" is to treat God frivolously, with disrespect and insincerity. Nowadays it's common to hear the name of God or his Son Jesus Christ used casually or as a curse. But this is a serious sin. "The Lord will not hold anyone guiltless who misuses his name" (v. 7).

B. Someone might try to downplay his misuse of God's name by saying, "Oh, I didn't mean anything by it." But that's just the point! When we speak of God, we should mean something by it. According to Jewish tradition, the scribes who copied the Scriptures were so careful to revere God's name, even if a king addressed them while they were writing down the name of God, they were to ignore the king completely.

C. How can we develop more reverent speech? It's hard to do (James 3:1-12), but not impossible with God's help. Here's a fivefold action plan:
1. *Wise up.* Acknowledge that this is a serious issue. It's easy to adopt the speech patterns of others around us instead of recognizing our responsibility to live differently as Christians. Face it: God cares how we use our tongues (Matthew 12:34-37).
2. *Reach out.* Ask others to help you. Find a trusted family member or friend who will hold you accountable and point out any irreverent speech patterns you've developed.

3. *Fill up.* Fill your mind with wholesome, faith-building words and music. Talk with others who exemplify purity of speech in their lives.
4. *Look up.* Read Scripture. Pray. "Set your minds on things above" (Colossians 3:2). Ask God to fill your speech with wisdom and grace (Colossians 4:4-6).
5. *Speak out.* Be honest with friends and family about your desire to discipline your own speech, and approach them with loving reminders when they use offensive speech.

II. A SCHEDULE THAT INCLUDES REST: RESPECT FOR GOD'S DAY

A. "Remember the Sabbath Day by keeping it holy" (v. 8). This Commandment encourages us to follow a healthy, balanced lifestyle. It affirms the value of work ("Six days you shall labor," v. 9). But it also underscores the necessity of rest ("the seventh day is a Sabbath to the Lord your God. On it you shall not do any work" (v. 10).

B. In a busy culture like ours, this may be one of the toughest Commandments to understand and apply. Excessive rest leads to laziness, but inadequate rest leads to craziness! God expects us to schedule time in our week to rejuvenate our bodies, refresh our spirits, relax our minds, and refocus our hearts on worship.

C. The Jews observed the Sabbath on the seventh day of the week (our Saturday), but under the inspired guidance of Jesus' apostles, the early church met on the first day of the week (the Lord's Day) to study, break bread, pray, give, and enjoy fellowship together (Acts 2:42; 20:7; 1 Corinthians 16:1, 2). This is the only one of the Ten Commandments not specifically repeated in the New Testament as binding upon Christians. In fact, Scripture specifically warns Christians not to judge one another based on Sabbath observance (Romans 14:5-8; Colossians 2:16). Yet Jesus is Lord of the Sabbath, and he gave mankind this principle to benefit us (Mark 2:27, 28).

D. Does your lifestyle include the right balance of work, worship, and rest? Despite our sins and failures, Jesus still beckons us to come to him. And when we do, we will find rest for our souls (Matthew 11:28, 29).

ILLUSTRATIONS

Meaningful names. In Bible times, names were considered quite significant. Benjamin's name meant "son of my right hand," which pointed to his close relationship with his father, Jacob (Genesis 35:18). Barnabas's name meant "Son of Encouragement," which aptly pictured the way he built others up (Acts 4:36). Jesus' name means "the Lord saves" (Matthew 1:21). Blessed be the name of the Lord!

Four-letter words. Why not replace profanity with some better four-letter words like love, home, kind, pray, help, care, rest, heal, and obey?

Godly Values: Honor God by Valuing Life

Exodus 20:12, 13

Since he is "the living God" and the author of life, God cares deeply about human life. Not only did he create all life; he took special delight in the people he created in his image (Genesis 1:26-31). He still knits babies together in their mothers' wombs (Psalm 139:13). He still detests "hands that shed innocent blood" (Proverbs 6:17). Jesus came to save lives, not to destroy them (see Luke 6:9).

Likewise, God wants us to care deeply about human life across the entire spectrum from infancy to death, from conception to the grave. To be people of integrity, we need to honor God by valuing life.

I. HONOR THOSE WHO GAVE US LIFE.

A. The fifth of the Ten Commandments reads, "Honor your father and your mother" (v. 12). As the apostle Paul notes (Ephesians 6:1-3), this is the first of the Commandments that includes a promise: "so that you may live long in the land the Lord your God is giving you." Healthy family relationships bring many blessings. When children honor their mothers and fathers . . .

1. It brings joy to their parents (Proverbs 23:24, 25).
2. It increases the likelihood that the children will avoid some of sin's harm and thus live longer, more productive lives (Proverbs 2:1-11).
3. It models healthy relationships and promotes stability in the church and in society as a whole (1 Timothy 3:5; 5:1, 2).

B. What does it mean to honor your parents? Admittedly, some parents make this quite difficult! But the basic principle still applies. Young children should obey their parents in the Lord, "for this is right"—not just when we think they're right (Ephesians 6:1). Even when we're grown up and have established our own independent households, our love for our parents demonstrates our love for God (1 Timothy 5:4-8).

C. If your parents have neglected or abused you, it will require extra effort and extra grace from God to fulfill this Commandment. While it's sometimes necessary to establish some healthy boundaries, with God's help, we all can strive to honor our parents by . . .

1. Appreciating them. They gave us life.
2. Learning from them. They have wisdom to impart.
3. Forgiving them. They aren't perfect.

4. Communicating with them. They can't read our minds.
5. Accepting them. They are who they are, not necessarily what we'd like them to be. Try to see them from God's point of view. He sees their weaknesses and their mistakes, but he also sees their potential for what they can be.
6. Praying for them. God can help them when no one else can.

II. HONOR GOD BY PROTECTING LIFE.

A. The sixth of the Ten Commandments says, "You shall not murder" (v. 13). Sometimes killing involves a direct act that takes a person's life: murder, suicide, abortion, infanticide. Other kinds of "killing" are more subtle, but just as vicious: spiteful words (Matthew 5:21, 22), jealous anger, hateful attitudes (1 John 3:12-15).

B. Christians can show value for human life by . . .
1. Treating all people with proper respect (1 Peter 2:17).
2. Speaking up for the rights of unborn children, the elderly, the sick, and the mentally retarded.
3. Teaching the truth, while also reaching out in love with counseling and practical assistance to unwed mothers, troubled kids, the poor, and those who struggle with postabortion guilt.
4. Supporting Christian ministries that address needs like these on a daily basis.

C. Some great servants of God disobeyed this Commandment about valuing life. Moses himself killed a man (Exodus 2:11-14). David arranged for the death of Bathsheba's husband, Uriah (2 Samuel 11:14-17). Saul of Tarsus (Paul) gave approval to the tragic stoning of Stephen, and later continued to breathe out "murderous threats against the Lord's disciples" (Acts 8:1; 9:1). But thank God, in Christ there is forgiveness and new life even for someone who has been "a blasphemer and a persecutor and a violent man" (1 Timothy 1:12-16).

ILLUSTRATIONS

Strength to forgive. Oscar Wilde once said, "Children begin by loving their parents; as they grow older they judge them; sometimes they forgive them." Since God wants us to honor our parents, he also can give us grace and strength to forgive—even when we see our parents' faults.

The path of life. It's sobering—and a bit frightening—to realize how close most of us are to death on a daily basis. When you drive a car down a highway, one wrong turn of the steering wheel could put an oncoming vehicle directly into your path. God calls us to guard not only our own lives, but also the lives of others. Most important, we need to choose the way of spiritual safety. "The path of life leads upward for the wise to keep him from going down to the grave" (Proverbs 15:24).

Godly Respect:
Honor God Through Sexual Purity and Respect for Others' Property
Exodus 20:14, 15

Signs that say "Beware of Dog," "Keep Off the Grass," or "Wet Paint" can keep us out of trouble. Signs along the highway can keep us from causing an accident: "Keep Right," "Speed Limit 65," "No Left Turn." In spite of all the rules of the road, we call it a "freeway," not a "slaveway." It's the "highway," not the "low way." There would be chaos if nobody respected the boundaries and followed the rules of the road.

To become people of integrity, we need to respect God's "rules of the road." In Exodus 20:14, 15 we read two clear road signs that could be translated, "No Trespassing!" Both are unpopular but important guidelines about the importance of not tampering with that which is not your own. You may not have thought of them this way, but both of them deal with respect for others. God's warning sign about adultery reminds us to respect the integrity of marriage (our own as well as the marriages of others), while his warning about stealing reminds us to respect the property of others.

I. A WARNING SIGN ABOUT SEXUAL PURITY: "YOU SHALL NOT COMMIT ADULTERY" (v. 14).

A. This command sounds quite countercultural in a society where we're bombarded daily by unprecedented levels of discussion, confusion, perversion, and temptation about sexuality. God intends that human sexuality should be sacred and beautiful. He created Adam and Eve, and other married couples after them, to "cleave" to one another in love, to "become one flesh," to be "naked and not ashamed" (Genesis 2:24, 25). Song of Solomon is filled with the vivid imagery of married love. Marriage—including sexual intimacy—is a powerful illustration of Christ's perfect love for the church (Ephesians 5:22-33; Hebrews 13:4).

B. But the Bible also tells us the downside about what happens when, like a fire out of control, sexuality is misused and becomes destructive. Who gets hurt when this "road sign" is ignored? Loved ones in our families and churches get hurt. Our own bodies and spirits get hurt (Proverbs 6:32; 1 Corinthians 6:18-20).

C. There is a better way. We can be faithful before we marry by committing ourselves to remain celibate while single (1 Corinthians 7:1-9). We can be faithful *during* marriage by maintaining our commitment, honoring our vows, developing healthy habits of communication, building positive memories, avoiding unfaithful thoughts (Job 31:1; Matthew 5:27, 28), and sharing joys and hardships in an atmosphere of trust.

II. A WARNING SIGN ABOUT PERSONAL PROPERTY: "YOU SHALL NOT STEAL" (v. 15).

A. Stealing not only hurts the victim; it also hurts the thief (Proverbs 6:30, 31). It steals our integrity, corrupts our sense of honor, and weakens our determination to earn our daily bread (Ephesians 4:28).

B. We need to avoid subtle forms of stealing such as gossip (which steals another person's reputation), cheating at school (which steals another student's work), dishonest business practices (which cheat customers or clients), excessive debts (which defraud our creditors), and plagiarism (which steals another person's ideas). Stingy folks even rob God when they refuse to give what he has asked them to give (Malachi 3:8-10).

C. The good news? God's grace is sufficient to save us from all our sins—including sexual immorality and stealing—if we come to Christ in faith and accept the cleansing only he can provide (1 Corinthians 6:9-11). Through repentance, we turn from sinful relationships and habits that have moved us off God's highway. In baptism, we receive "the forgiveness of sins and the gift of the Holy Spirit" (Acts 2:38). Let's follow God's road signs. He alone can keep us safe.

ILLUSTRATIONS

Long-term marriage. Years ago someone sent a little poem to advice columnist Ann Landers that said, "I met him, I liked him, I loved him, I let him, I lost him." Later a man sent another poem of his own: "I saw her, I liked her, I loved her, I wanted her, I asked her. She said 'no.' I married her. After 60 years, I still have her."

Marital harmony. When my daughter Mindy was 11, she told me, "I have my life all planned out." She paused for a moment, then said thoughtfully, "I sure hope my husband will agree with it!"

Godly Relationships:
Honor God by the Way You Treat Your Neighbors
Exodus 20:16, 17

We hear a lot about relationships today. But sadly, many relationships with friends and family are less than healthy and less than satisfying. How can we build better relationships with others? The last two of the Ten Commandments give us a couple of bedrock truths that are too important to overlook. Both of these principles tell us how to treat our neighbors.

I. BE TRUTHFUL IN WHAT WE SAY.

A. "You shall not give false testimony against your neighbor" (v. 16). Are any of the Ten Commandments violated more often than this one? Our culture puts so much "spin" on the truth, we're in danger of "spinning out of control."

B. Lying has become so commonplace we almost accept it as a fact of life. Why are we tempted to lie?
1. To get ourselves out of trouble or to cover up mistakes. ("Sorry, Professor, the computer lost my homework.")
2. To avoid hurting someone's feelings. ("Oh, I really like your new haircut.")
3. To manipulate public opinion or gain advantages over others. ("Vote for me and I'll bring lots of government money back to this district.")

C. Some call lying "spin," but God calls it sin. Lying is the devil's native language (John 8:44); it shouldn't be ours. It insults the God of truth, who never lies (Hebrews 6:18). He desires "truth in the inner parts" of our lives (Psalm 51:6). Lying hurts others (Proverbs 25:18). It even leads us to deceive ourselves (Jeremiah 17:9; James 1:22). Lying ultimately deserves the punishment of God. (See Acts 5:1-11; Revelation 22:15.)

D. We can overcome dishonesty by committing ourselves to truthfulness, even in small matters. We can stop engaging in gossip, insincere flattery, and hypocritical actions that belie the truths we claim to believe. "Therefore each of you must put off falsehood and speak truthfully to his neighbor, for we are all members of one body" (Ephesians 4:25).

II. BE CONTENT WITH WHAT WE HAVE.

A. "You shall not covet" (v. 17). Covetousness not only makes us envy what others own; it also makes us fail to appreciate what we ourselves own. If we learn to be content, we'll be less likely to covet. (See Philippians 4:11, 12; 1 Timothy 6:6-10.)

B. Perhaps your neighbors don't own a "manservant or maidservant," an "ox or donkey" as people did in Moses' day (v. 17). However, this Commandment still applies. Do you ever long to possess someone else's "house," or his "wife," "or anything that belongs to your neighbor" (v. 17)? Instead of longing to have our neighbors' belongings, we need to keep our lives free from the love of money and be content with what we have (Hebrews 13:5).

C. Our friends and families know whether we're truthful in what we say and content with what we have. Honest lives filled with godliness, contentment, and peace are winsome to others. If we demonstrate that we're people of integrity who can be fully trusted, we'll "make the teaching about God our Savior attractive" to a watching world (Titus 2:6-10).

ILLUSTRATIONS

Enough, already! One time I asked my wife, Candy, to write down on a piece of paper some of her suggestions for improving our family life. We're quite happy together on the whole, so I was surprised to see that she had written down a rather lengthy list ("Spend more evenings at home," "Go on dates more often," that kind of thing). By the time I finished reading her list, I was grateful for two blessings: (1) I was glad God gave me such a wise wife, and (2) I was glad Candy didn't write an even longer list! We may feel some similar emotions as we come to the end of our study of the Ten Commandments. I'm glad God gave us these guiding principles that offer us a prescription for integrity. It's also a relief when we finally come to the end of the list! We haven't obeyed these laws perfectly, not to mention the rest of God's laws. Praise God, we are saved by grace!

Nothing to complain about. One of the rules of home ownership is that no matter what you do or how much money you spend, there's always something else to repair or update—from a leaky roof to broken appliances, to worn-out carpets to leaky water pipes. Cars are even worse—and auto repairs are no small problem to someone as "mechanically challenged" as I am. But I began to view such annoyances differently when I visited Ethiopia. There I ate with a family who lived in a dirt-floored hut made of mud, tree limbs, and grass. They owned no car, but they seemed content and were remarkably hospitable. In comparison with the rest of the world, most Americans have little to complain about and a lot for which to be thankful. Gratitude, not greed, should fill our hearts.

New Insights From the Old Law

John 1:17; Galatians 3:10-14

If you were President of the United States, what would you do to make our nation stronger, safer, more godly and just? If you were elected to Congress and could develop new laws that would benefit your fellow citizens, what new legislation would you propose?

Let's take this a step further. What if no written laws presently existed, and you were starting from scratch? What if you had to write new laws for a whole nation of people? How would you ensure that the people would be governed justly, in a way that honored God?

The Bible says, "For the law was given through Moses; grace and truth came through Jesus Christ" (John 1:17). To this day, many of the laws of the Western world are based on a code of right and wrong God revealed to Moses more than 3,000 years ago. Why did God give the law through Moses?

I. GOD'S LAWS BENEFIT HIS PEOPLE.

A. God has our best interests at heart. Some of his rules may be hard for us to understand, but "his commands are not burdensome" (1 John 5:3). The law of Moses set down rules for dealing with serious crimes like theft, arson, perjury, and manslaughter (Exodus 22:1-6; 23:1-3; Deuteronomy 19:4-7). It also provided helpful, practical guidelines for dealing with everyday problems like caring for widows and orphans, following fair lending practices, helping neighbors locate missing property, showing respect for the elderly, following honest business practices, following safe building practices—even helping newlyweds get off to a good start during their first year of marriage (Exodus 22:22-26; 23:4, 5; Leviticus 19:32-36; Deuteronomy 22:8; 24:5). Even the food laws, which specified what animals the people could eat, protected the Israelites from disease.

B. According to Jesus, all of God's laws hinge on two basic principles: love for God and love for our neighbors. These foundational principles underlay the Ten Commandments (the first 4 deal with love for God, the last 6 with love for others). Love motivates us to fulfill God's intentions: "to act justly and to love mercy and to walk humbly with [our] God" (Micah 6:8). God gave his laws for our good.

II. GOD'S LAWS POINT US TO CHRIST.

A. God's laws are good, but by themselves, they aren't enough to save us. None of us have kept all of God's laws (Romans 3:23; James 2:8-11; 1 John 1:8-10). In fact, it's precisely because God gave us his law that we know what's right and wrong, and we know how far we've fallen short (Romans 7:7-12).

B. Because we've broken God's laws, we deserve his judgment. If we rely on our own goodness for salvation, we fall under the curse of guilt and condemnation (Galatians 3:10). But because Christ came, we can receive the free gift of eternal life (Romans 6:23). Christ kept the law perfectly, for he never sinned. But he "redeemed us from the curse of the law by becoming a curse for us" (Galatians 3:13). God's law pronounced a solemn curse upon anyone who was "hung on a tree" (Deuteronomy 21:23), but when Jesus carried our sins in his body on the cross, he endured the punishment we deserved (1 Peter 2:24).

C. God's laws can guide our lives, but laws alone can't save a sinner's soul. The law "was put in charge to lead us to Christ that we might be justified by faith" (Galatians 3:24). We're saved when we accept God's "grace and truth" that came through Christ, place our faith in him, and unite with him in baptism (Galatians 3:16-29).

D. Even Moses himself pointed others to Jesus. (See John 5:46.) He said the day would come when God would raise up a great prophet from among his people, and that the people should listen to him (Deuteronomy 18:18). When Jesus was transfigured, God said of him (in the presence of Moses, the lawgiver), "This is my Son, whom I love; with him I am well pleased. Listen to him!" (Matthew 17:5).

ILLUSTRATIONS

The school bus driver. To supplement his income as a farmer, my grandfather drove a school bus for a couple of years. I have fond memories of the way he sometimes let my brothers and me play in it when it was parked in his driveway for the weekend. A bus driver has an important job. His role is not to teach the students, but to provide a place of safety and discipline while he transports them safely to their teachers. Similarly, the Law of Moses played an important role by guiding God's people. But the Law alone doesn't save us; it brings us to Christ, the Master Teacher, so that we can find salvation in him.

"For your own good." Parents often explain disciplinary actions to their children by saying, "This is for your own good." When you're on the receiving end, though, discipline doesn't always feel "good"! God our Creator understands us better than we even understand ourselves. His discipline is truly "for our good" (Hebrews 12:7-11).

The Last Straw

Exodus 5–11

Did you ever come to the place in your life when you said, "That's the last straw"? When your get-up-and-go long ago got up and went? When your "drive" has shifted into "park"? When we face painful problems, it's tempting to wonder, "How can I endure another day?"

In *Where Is God When It Hurts?* Philip Yancey points out that pain isn't "God's great mistake"; it's "the gift nobody wants." No one enjoys physical suffering, whether it's a temporary aggravation (like a scrape or a bruise) or a long-term sorrow (like a debilitating illness). Nor do we appreciate spiritual suffering, even though our faith and character grow when we endure hardships (James 1:2-4). More than 3,000 years ago, the people of Israel endured struggles not unlike the kind we face today.

I. THEIR ENEMIES MISTREATED THEM.

A. Fresh from his wilderness encounter with God, Moses and his brother Aaron confronted the king of Egypt with an amazing demand: God wanted Pharaoh to free the slaves (5:1-3). But instead of granting Moses' request, Pharaoh increased the Hebrews' workload. The slaves used straw to reinforce the bricks they made of mud. But now Pharaoh demanded that they still produce the same daily quota of bricks, but they'd have to find their own straw (5:4-16). That would be sort of like saying to an auto worker, "You have to keep turning out the same number of cars each day, but we aren't going to provide any steel for you to use. You have to find your own!" As if their lifestyle weren't already harsh enough, the Hebrew slaves now became scavengers, searching the land of Egypt not only for long-stemmed pieces of straw but even the stubble—short, scratchy stems left over from the harvest. It must have added to their frustration when, amid their miserable workdays, they were labeled "lazy" by Pharaoh (5:17, 18).

B. Enemies are an unpleasant fact of life. Even in the comforting Psalm 23, David doesn't expect that God will completely eliminate his enemies, but that the Lord will prepare him a table in their presence. God nourishes us and gives us strength to keep going when adversaries are unreasonable and demanding. Not only that, in Christ we can even find power to love our enemies and overcome evil with good (Matthew 5:43-48; Romans 12:17-21).

35

II. THEIR FRIENDS MISUNDERSTOOD THEM.

A. You might expect your enemies to mistreat you, but it really hurts when your friends misunderstand. Moses and Aaron soon found themselves confronted by the Israelite foremen, who complained bitterly, "You have made us a stench to Pharaoh" (5:21). These men didn't hesitate to make their feelings known: "Moses, this stinks! And you're supposed to be our friend and our leader?"

B. Few hurts compare with the pain of having a close friend misunderstand you or accuse you of wrongdoing. David wrote about this hurt (Psalm 55:12-14, 20, 21), and Jesus was well-acquainted with it as well. Not only was he betrayed by his friend Judas; in a larger sense, "he came to that which was his own, but his own did not receive him" (John 1:11). If your relationships with others have left you thinking, "That's the last straw," remember: Jesus is a "friend who sticks closer than a brother" (Proverbs 18:24).

III. THEIR GOD DID NOT ABANDON THEM.

A. At first, Moses felt abandoned by God. He cried out in frustration (5:22, 23). He reverted back to his old habit of focusing on his inability as a speaker (6:12, 30). No doubt he felt discouraged when the suffering Israelites refused to listen (6:9) and Pharaoh's heart continued to grow harder (7:13, 22; 8:15, 19, 32, etc.).

B. But God was still with Moses and his people. His covenant promises were still true (6:1-4). He still listened to their groans and cared about their suffering (6:5). He still had the power to free his people, but he would do this on his own timetable—after sending the 10 plagues. In the end, more than half a million Israelites marched victoriously out of Egypt, carrying with them silver and gold and clothing their Egyptian captors gave them (12:33-42). God was strong and faithful—even when his people were down to the last straw.

ILLUSTRATIONS

Honest to God. During my days in Bible college, I went through a period when God seemed distant and prayer was difficult for me. I went to one of my professors and said, "There are times I just don't feel like praying, or I don't know what to say." The professor replied, "Well, then, just level with God. Tell him how you feel. Be honest, just as you would with any personal friend." I said, "But I wouldn't want God to know I'm angry and upset." Kindly the wise professor responded, "God already knows you're angry and upset! But you need to talk to him about it." Nothing we tell God surprises him. But honest prayer helps us sense the loving concern of the one who promised to reward those who earnestly seek him (Hebrews 11:6).

Time flies. We often say time flies, but there are, after all, different ways to fly. Sometimes time flies swiftly and purposefully, like an eagle. Other times, it limps along like a wounded duck. It can fly with the smoothness and power of a 747, but sometimes it's like the Goodyear blimp hovering quietly overhead. Whether we soar or sputter, God can keep us flying onward if we trust in him.

Christ, Our Passover

Exodus 12:1-13

Once a year, in early spring, families all over the world eat a special meal consisting of foods like parsley, a hard-boiled egg, ground horseradish, a mixture of chopped apples with cinnamon and nuts, and wafers of matzo or unleavened bread. It's the Passover meal, and each item on the menu has a symbolic meaning to the Jewish people. For example, the brownish mixture of apples and nuts symbolizes the mortar the Hebrews used to make bricks when they were slaves in Egypt. Exodus 12 details how the Passover meal began, and explains the symbolism God intended for this special meal.

I. WHAT GOD'S PEOPLE DID

A. They participated in a family meal (vv. 1-4). The Passover wasn't eaten alone; it was eaten in fellowship with others. Families too small to consume an entire lamb would combine with another household. God structured this important spiritual event around a family meal or a meal to be shared with neighbors. Likewise, at the center of Christian worship is a common meal (the Lord's Supper) eaten together with other believers in remembrance of the Lord Jesus (1 Corinthians 10:16, 17; 11:23-26).

B. They sacrificed a flawless lamb. The Passover lamb served as a vivid "type" or illustration of Christ. A year-old male "without defect" (v. 5) would have reached the prime of his physical maturity, just as sinless Jesus was crucified in his prime at age 33. The lamb was chosen ahead of time (vv. 5, 6), just as "Christ, a lamb without blemish or defect" . . . "was chosen before the creation of the world" (1 Peter 1:19, 20). The lamb was roasted whole (vv. 7-10) without any of its bones being broken (v. 46), just as Jesus' bones remained unbroken when he died on the cross (John 19:31-37).

C. They ate unspoiled bread, "made without yeast" (v. 8). Normally the Hebrews ate bread that, like today's sourdough, was made by adding a small lump of leavening to the rest of the dough. Quite often in the Bible, leaven or yeast symbolizes the influence of evil (Mark 8:14-16; 1 Corinthians 5:6-8). Likewise, the unleavened bread Christians eat during Communion reminds us of the pure, unspoiled body of Christ. Unlike the Hebrews who had to eat in haste (vv. 11, 39), we need to take time to pause and reflect on the significance of the bread and the cup that accompanies it (1 Corinthians 11:27-32).

II. WHAT GOD DID

A. God performed an act of judgment. He passed through Egypt to strike down the firstborn in every household (v. 12). Like the rest of the plagues, this final plague was intended to bring "judgment on all the gods of Egypt." The thought of divine judgment makes people uncomfortable, but it is a reality nonetheless. As if to underscore his authority, God adds, "I am the Lord" (v. 12). God's justice was done then; it will be done again at the end of time (Revelation 20:11-15).

B. But God also performed an act of mercy. He passed over the houses where the blood of the lamb had been applied (v. 13). That dark night, the lamb's blood spelled the difference between life and death. It was messy to kill a lamb and smear its blood on the front door of a house. "Without the shedding of blood there is no forgiveness" (Hebrews 9:22). God didn't say, "If you're perfect, I'll pass over you." He said, "When I see the blood, I will pass over you."

III. WHAT THE BLOOD OF CHRIST DOES

A. The Passover vividly portrays the suffering and death of Jesus Christ. Thank God, we don't have to try to atone for our own sins, "for Christ, our Passover lamb, has been sacrificed" (1 Corinthians 5:7).

B. In Egypt, the blood of the lamb was the way God distinguished the saved from the unsaved. A final judgment is coming, when our social status, our riches, and our education won't matter. It *will* matter whether we've had the blood of Christ applied to our souls. Some may disbelieve it, modern theologians may ridicule it, and we may not fully understand it, but there's still power in the blood!

ILLUSTRATIONS

Giving blood. Have you ever given blood? The folks at the blood bank try to make the experience as pleasant as possible. You lie on a couch, and afterward they give you a snack. I have to admit, I don't enjoy the process. For some reason, it usually takes the nurse a while to locate my veins, and my blood doesn't flow very freely. I guess it's true: I do have some stubbornness in my veins! Instinctively, we seem to understand that blood represents the very life of a person (see Leviticus 17:14). Aren't you glad Jesus willingly "freed us from our sins by his blood" (Revelation 1:5)?

Lamb of God. It's not unusual to use animals to illustrate certain qualities we find in people. Jesus compared Herod to a fox (Luke 13:31, 32), false prophets to wolves (Matthew 7:15), and his followers to doves (Matthew 10:16). People say, "He eats like a pig. She's as busy as a bee. He's as mean as a junkyard dog!" But John the Baptist found the perfect way to describe the perfect Christ: "Look, the Lamb of God" (John 1:29). Christ fulfilled the vivid symbolism of the Passover and prophecies like Isaiah 53. He is the ultimate sacrifice for sin (Hebrews 10:11-14).

Overcoming Spiritual Droughts

Exodus 15:19-27

The Christian life isn't one big spiritual high. Sometimes it's more like a spiritual "dry." Do you ever feel you have little to give, little joy in going to church, little desire to serve? Do you ever find yourself doubting like Thomas, suffering like Job, feeling busy and distracted like Martha? Do you ever long to feel close to God again, like the psalmist who sang, "As the deer pants for streams of water, so my soul pants for you, O God" (Psalm 42:1)?

How can we handle our spiritual droughts? Just as the Israelites began wandering in the wilderness on their way to the promised land, they went through a dry time. We can learn some lessons from them about how to deal with our own spiritual dry spells.

I. DON'T FORGET WHAT GOD DID FOR YOU IN THE PAST (vv. 19-22).

A. God had parted the Red Sea and thwarted the Egyptian army's pursuit (v. 19). Moses' sister Miriam (who was about 90 years old by now, but still had some vitality!) led thousands of women in a spirited song of praise to the Lord (vv. 20, 21). The people were filled with joy!

B. But if the Israelites thought they'd sing and dance all the way to the Promised Land, they were wrong. Almost immediately, they traveled three days in the desert without finding water (v. 22). No doubt they had carried some water with them from Egypt; but now in the heat of the desert, accompanied by families with little children and livestock to feed and water, intense joy quickly gave way to intense hardship. The thrill of following God was swallowed up by the dry desert of daily survival. Often our toughest trials come soon after our biggest victories. (For example, immediately after Jesus was baptized, he went into the wilderness of temptation.) During the dry times, we need to recall God's faithfulness to us in the past.

II. DON'T MAGNIFY YOUR PRESENT PROBLEMS (vv. 23, 24).

A. The water at Marah was bitter (vv. 23, 24). Evidently, it was filled with bad-tasting minerals. But at least it was water! If it means survival, a thirsty man will drink almost anything. I worked at a church camp where the drinking water tasted like sulfur. The campers called it "egg-water." But on a hot summer day, that bad-tasting water was better than nothing!

B. The Israelites were magnifying their problems and making them appear bigger than they really were. Likewise, we sometimes wallow in self-pity, exaggerate our hardships, and overlook our blessings. (Compare Hebrews 12:4.)

III. DON'T OVERLOOK GOD'S SOLUTIONS (vv. 25, 26).

A. The Lord provided a miraculous water softener! When Moses threw a piece of wood into the water, the water became sweet (v. 25). The Israelites' thirst tested their faith, but it also introduced them to some solutions if they would heed God's "decree and law."

B. Even in "dry" times:

1. You can pray. "Moses cried out to the Lord" (v. 25). God's Spirit helps when we don't know what to say (Romans 8:26, 27).
2. You can obey. "If you listen carefully . . . and do what is right" (v. 26). When you're in a spiritual drought, don't give into temptation and do foolish things you'll later regret. Don't cheat on your spouse, desert your kids, squander your money, quit your job, give up on church, or throw away your faith.
3. You can rely on God's goodness. "For I am the Lord, who heals you."

IV. DON'T GIVE UP TOO SOON (v. 27).

A. Soon the Israelites left a bitter place and moved to a better place. Elim sounds like a Florida beach, complete with 12 springs and 70 palm trees (v. 27)—a refreshing place to rest and drink. Remarkably, Elim was only about a day's journey from Marah on foot. The people felt discouraged and bitter, but God's remedy was only one day away!

B. When you feel like you're at the end of your rope, your friends have let you down, your family has disappointed you, and you wonder if it's worth it all, you can still find strength in Jesus who said, "If anyone is thirsty, let him come to me and drink" (John 7:37).

ILLUSTRATIONS

The party's over. On our daughter Mindy's thirteenth birthday, our family acquired a Cocker Spaniel named Herby. My daughter Mindy greeted the dog with great enthusiasm. It was fun to romp and play with a brand new puppy. But after a few days, Mindy realized dog ownership has its responsibilities as well as its privileges. The joy of playing with Herby diminished with the daily feedings, walks, and clean-ups, and occasional trips to the vet. Though we'd like for life to be a pleasant romp, it's often difficult. We need faith that's tough enough to endure even when the fun is gone.

Abundant life. After *Saturday Night Live* comedian John Belushi died of a drug overdose, one of his friends explained, "John always believed in living his life to the fullest." Could anyone really believe that the kind of wild partying that led to Belushi's tragic death was "living life to the fullest"? Jesus gives abundant life (John 10:10). Don't settle for a substitute—especially a deadly one.

God Will Take Care of You

Exodus 16:9-35

God has promised to meet our needs "according to his glorious riches in Christ Jesus" (Philippians 4:19). But sometimes our circumstances test our faith in God's ability to provide.

Have you ever faced a time of financial hardship when you wondered whether (and how) God would really take care of you? Have you ever wondered, "Where will we get our daily bread?" As the ancient Israelites wandered in the wilderness, they wondered where their next meal was coming from; but God proved faithful and he met their needs.

I. THE LORD IS GOD: HONOR HIM (vv. 9-12).

A. The Israelites had been grumbling about their lack of food (vv. 1-8). The whole time, however, God had been providing for them. He knew their need and was concerned about them.

B. But their greatest need was not something to eat; it was Someone to worship. "Man does not live on bread alone" (Deuteronomy 8:3; Matthew 4:4).

II. THE LORD'S BLESSINGS SOMETIMES COME IN SURPRISING FORMS: RECOGNIZE THEM (vv. 13-15).

A. When God sent manna from Heaven, at first the people weren't even sure what it was. The very word *manna* means "What is it?"

B. Has God ever met your need in a way that surprised you? Even now, are there blessings you simply need to open your eyes and recognize?

III. THE LORD PROVIDES FOR OUR NEEDS, NOT OUR GREEDS: OBEY HIM (vv. 16-30).

A. God provided manna every day—just enough for each person to gather what he or she needed. However, to ensure that the people would trust him to provide, the Lord commanded the people not to gather *more* than they needed. The only exception? On the day before the Sabbath, they could gather enough for two days, so they wouldn't have to work on the Sabbath Day. Sadly, the people disobeyed these commands and tried to hoard more manna than they needed. Their selfish acts proved futile, for the extra manna they gathered "was full of maggots and began to smell" (v. 20).

41

B. There are many noble purposes for working and making money. Through our work we use our God-given gifts, provide for the needs of our families, acquire goods we can share with others in need, and earn the respect of our neighbors (1 Peter 4:10, 11; 1 Timothy 5:8; Ephesians 4:28; 1 Thessalonians 4:11, 12). But we shouldn't work because of greed or a desire to hoard our wealth. "Do not wear yourself out to get rich; have the wisdom to show restraint. Cast but a glance at riches, and they are gone . . ." (Proverbs 23:4, 5).

IV. THE LORD HAS A LONG TRACK RECORD OF FAITHFULNESS: TRUST HIM (vv. 31-35).

A. The daily bread arrived consistently—every day (except Sabbaths) for 40 years. It even tasted good—with a hint of honey. Its presence in the tabernacle offered a lasting testimony to God's provision.

B. Christians sometimes endure times of want, along with times of plenty (2 Corinthians 11:27; Philippians 4:11-13). But we can trust God to provide our daily bread until we reach that promised land where hunger and thirst will be no more (Revelation 21:6).

ILLUSTRATIONS

Walking with God. The Christian life is often described as "walking with God." Walking is an appropriate metaphor for spiritual growth. When we walk, we move forward. When we walk with another person, we must keep in step, adopting the same pace and going in the same direction. And walking means we're always on the verge of losing our balance as we lift one foot and put it ahead of the other. When we walk with the Lord, we stay in fellowship with him and go the same direction he's going; all the while, we must trust him even when it feels a bit off-balance to take another step.

Not by bread alone. Honestly, which do we value more: the Word of God or our next meal? Which do we think about more often? Which would we miss more if we had to do without it for a day? Has there ever been a time when you truly had to trust God for your daily food? What does our attitude about food say about our priorities—and about our concern for the world's many hungry people? Could fasting be a useful discipline to help us put food back into its proper perspective?

Lifting Up Our Leaders

Exodus 17:8-13

Leading God's people can be rewarding, fulfilling, enjoyable—even thrilling at times. But ask anyone who's been involved in church leadership very long, and you'll find out it also can be frustrating, draining, difficult, and exhausting as well. Despite our best intentions, many servants of God are tempted to grow "weary in well doing" (Galatians 6:9, *King James Version*).

Even a strong leader like Moses needed others around him to help bear the load—to lift up his hands and encourage him in his work.

I. TIRED HANDS

A. At this early point in their wilderness journey, the Israelites weren't very well-prepared for war. They were newly-liberated slaves, accustomed to making bricks, not fighting battles. They had little choice but to fight, however, for the Amalekites grew nervous and attacked the approaching throng of Israelites. Seeing that the Israelites couldn't win the battle by their own strength alone, Moses depended on the one thing that had already gotten him through many tight spots before: the power of God, symbolized by the wooden staff he held in his hands (vv. 8-11). God had performed many miracles with this staff in the past, along with Aaron's staff as well (Exodus 4:1-5, 17; 7:8-12; 8:16; 14:16). Now the staff was the key to success in battle. Whatever other supernatural power the staff brought to the situation, no doubt it rallied and encouraged the troops in the valley below when they saw their leader on top of the hill with the staff of God held high.

B. But despite his great strength, Moses was a mortal man. His hands grew tired. Even the greatest of leaders have areas of weakness. Moses needed help.

II. FAITHFUL HELPERS

A. Two men came to Moses' aid (v. 12). One was Moses' brother Aaron, who had already served as his faithful coworker for some time. The other was a man named Hur, who evidently was a friend and companion of Aaron, and respected by the people (Exodus 24:14).

B. They took several practical steps to help Moses:
1. They noticed Moses' weariness. (Not everyone is sensitive enough to real-

ize that leaders have needs of their own.)

    2. They helped Moses rest. (They put a rock under him so he could sit down. Some of today's leaders may need a breather, a day off, or a vacation.)

    3. They stood by Moses' side all day. (Their very presence must have encouraged him.)

    4. They held up Moses' hands. (In the process, their own hands must have grown weary, but they were willing to help.)

C. The result? Victory for God's people (v. 13). Everyone benefited when God's leader was strong and supported by others.

D. Scripture says, "Carry each other's burdens, and in this way you will fulfill the law of Christ" (Galatians 6:2). Even our leaders have burdens to bear. How can we be faithful helpers to our church's leaders (elders, ministers, teachers, parents, youth sponsors, and others whose hands sometimes grow weary from their tasks)?

    1. Respect them (1 Thessalonians 5:12, 13).

    2. Honor them and be generous with them (1 Timothy 5:17, 18).

    3. Treat them fairly—confront them directly when they are wrong, but guard them against gossip and false accusations (1 Timothy 5:19-21).

    4. Follow their example and imitate their faith (Hebrews 13:7).

    5. Obey them and submit to them; make their work a joy, not a burden (Hebrews 13:17).

    6. Greet them cheerfully (Hebrews 13:24).

    7. Make sure their needs are met (1 Corinthians 9:7-14; Galatians 6:6).

ILLUSTRATIONS

Power lines. E. M. Bounds, known for his writings about prayer, once noted that church members who pray for their leaders are like the wooden utility poles that hold up electric lines and enable the power to flow freely.

Behind the scenes. A preacher in one of today's churches may seem to do impressive work, but consider this: Without someone operating the sound system, no one would hear the preacher. Without others tending the nursery, families with young children might not come to hear the preacher. Without the parking lot attendants and the ushers, the custodians and the Communion servers, and all the other workers who do their part, the preacher might not have the opportunity to do his work. Ministry is a team effort. We should honor our up-front leaders, but never devalue the work that goes on behind the scenes. It is God's work too!

A Covenant With God

Exodus 24:1-8

When we hear the word covenant, we may think of a contract. But today, we sign contracts in order to protect ourselves from others. In biblical times, however, a covenant usually meant something more positive. Like a peace treaty, it established the terms of agreement by which each party agreed to advance the best interests of the other.

I. BIBLICAL COVENANTS

A. Biblical covenants had four basic elements: parties (the persons involved), terms (the actions and promises required of each person involved), promises (the rewards for abiding by the terms of the covenant), and penalties (the consequences of neglecting or disobeying the covenant).

B. Examples of biblical covenants among human beings:
1. Covenants concerning personal issues: Isaac and Abimelech (Genesis 26:28-30); Jacob and Laban (Genesis 31:43-54); Rahab and the spies (Joshua 2:12-21; 6:25); David and Jonathan (1 Samuel 18:3; 20:8; 23:18).
2. The marriage covenant (Malachi 2:13, 14).
3. Treaties with kings, tribes, or other groups (Deuteronomy 7:2; 2 Samuel 5:3).
4. Usually covenant agreements like these involved some sort of solemn act that formally ratified the promises made: a shared meal (Genesis 31:54); the striking of hands (Ezra 10:19); the symbolic giving of a piece of personal property (Ruth 4:7); and the setting up of a stone (Genesis 31:45).

C. Examples of biblical covenants between God and human beings:
1. God is a covenant-making God (2 Chronicles 6:14). In all covenants between God and men, it is God who takes the initiative. He sets the terms. We do not dictate covenant terms to God. We can decide whether or not we will abide by the terms of the covenant, but God sets the terms.
2. God entered into covenants with Noah, symbolized by the rainbow (Genesis 6:18; 9:12, 13), Abraham, symbolized by circumcision (Genesis 15:5-18; 17:11), and Moses and the people of Israel, symbolized by Sabbath-keeping (Exodus 31:13-17).

II. THE OLD COVENANT

A. Where given? At Mt. Sinai, to Moses and the people of Israel (Exodus 24:1, 2).

45

B. Terms? The people promised to hear and obey the Word of God; God promised to make Israel his "treasured possession," "kingdom of priests" and "holy nation" (Exodus 19:3-6; 24:3, 4). Moses took several steps to confirm this covenant: he wrote down what God had said (v. 4); he built an altar and set up pillars, one for each of the tribes of Israel (v. 4); he offered animal sacrifices (vv. 5, 6); he read God's covenant laws to the people, and they promised to obey (v. 7); and he sprinkled blood on the people as a vivid reminder of the covenant (v. 8).

C. What was good about the old covenant? It clearly defined the boundaries of right and wrong (Romans 7:7). It provided a unified God-centered worldview, a godly framework for life (Joshua 1:8). It foreshadowed the blessings of God's new covenant relationship with his people. (For example, Exodus 12's Passover foreshadows the sacrifice of Christ, and Exodus 26's tabernacle illustrates our holy dwelling with God in Heaven—compare Hebrews 9:9, 10, 23-25.) The old covenant was a blessing from God, intended to teach and guide us and lead us to Christ (Romans 15:4; 1 Corinthians 10:11).

D. What was lacking in it? It brought awareness of sin, but not complete remission of it (Romans 7:14–8:4; Hebrews 10:4). It was designed to lead us to the Savior, not to be our Savior (Galatians 3:19-29). It resulted in death, not life, because people didn't keep it perfectly (1 Corinthians 15:56; Galatians 3:10).

III. THE NEW COVENANT

A. It was anticipated by the old covenant (Jeremiah 31:31-34; Ezekiel 37:26; Isaiah 42:6; Matthew 5:17, 18).

B. It is better than the old covenant (Hebrews 8:6-13; Colossians 2:16, 17):
1. International, not national (Colossians 3:11).
2. Emphasizes grace and truth, not just the law (John 1:17).
3. Written in the heart, not on stone (2 Corinthians 3:3).
4. Entered by spiritual birth, not physical (John 3:3-5).
5. Based on Christ's sacrifice on the cross, not the sacrifice of animals on altars (Hebrews 10:1-10).
6. Worship anywhere in spirit and truth, not just at a temple in Jerusalem (John 4:24; Acts 7:48).
7. Contains increasing glory, not fading glory (2 Corinthians 3:7-18).
8. Leads to life, not death (Colossians 2:13, 14).

ILLUSTRATION

Covenant meal. At the last supper Jesus called the cup his "blood of the covenant" (Matthew 26:28). Moses sprinkled blood on the people externally at Mt. Sinai (Exodus 24:8). But when we partake of the Lord's Supper and drink from the cup, we take the fruit of the vine internally and remember our covenant promises to the one who poured out his blood on the cross to forgive our sins.

Too Many Offerings

Exodus 35:20–36:7

Did you ever attend a worship service where the leaders interrupted the offering and said, "Please stop giving"? Have you ever seen a church budget where the problem was too much money available to do the Lord's work? What a great problem to have!

As the Israelites prepared to build a tabernacle for the worship of God, they encountered this very problem. There were too many offerings—more than enough resources—for the project. In many cases, the Israelites weren't faithful to the Lord. But in this case, we can learn a lot from their example about true stewardship and healthy giving.

I. THEY GAVE THEIR HEARTS (35:20, 21).

A. Good stewardship begins not with our wallets but with our wills, not with our bank accounts but with our beliefs, not with our money but with our minds.

B. In New Testament times, a group of Christians in the Greek province of Macedonia "gave themselves first to the Lord" and then their hearts overflowed in generous giving for the needs of others (2 Corinthians 8:1-5). God doesn't need our belongings, but he desires our obedience.

II. THEY GAVE THEIR POSSESSIONS (35:22-24, 27-29).

A. Sometimes a nonmonetary gift can even mean more than a check or cash. In the early church, believers sold property and gave the proceeds to the church, and people like Dorcas made useful items to give away in Jesus' name (Acts 2:45; 4:32-35; 9:36-39). What could you and I make, sell, or donate to help someone in need or as a way to contribute to another worthy cause?

B. Giving can be a source of joy not only for the receiver but also for the giver (2 Corinthians 9:6-15).

III. THEY GAVE THEIR ABILITIES (35:25, 26, 30–36:1).

A. "Each one should use whatever gift he has received to serve others, faithfully administering God's grace in its various forms" (1 Peter 4:10). Some gifts have to do with speaking or communicating the Word of God; other gifts involve practical acts of service (1 Peter 4:11). All gifts need to be used to glorify God and build up the body.

B. Can you serve God through your skill with a paintbrush, a mechanic's wrench, a musical instrument, a computer, or a basketball? Do you have a talent to offer in cooking, counseling, or carpentry? Can you teach children, take beautiful photographs, write poetry or thoughtful articles? What skills can you offer the Lord?

IV. THEY GAVE MORE THAN ENOUGH (36:2-7).

A. "And God is able to make all grace abound to you, so that in all things at all times, having all that you need, you will abound in every good work" (2 Corinthians 9:8).

B. He owns "the cattle on a thousand hills" (Psalm 50:10). He provides enough resources—even more than enough— for his people to accomplish great things if we will work together unselfishly. Are we willing to open our hands and open our hearts?

ILLUSTRATIONS

The color of money. Cash comes in different sizes, shapes, and colors, depending on the country of its issue. In biblical times, people used the shekel, the drachma, and the denarius. Today we use dollars, yen, pesos, pounds, marks, and other currency. But in every culture, money represents value and the power to purchase. And in every culture, it possesses a dangerous trait: if not properly submitted to the will of God, it becomes a competitor for the rightful role of God (Matthew 6:24; 1 Timothy 6:6-10).

Three books. A preacher friend of mine used to say, "It takes three books to build a great church: the Good Book (the Bible), the songbook (the hymnal) . . . and the pocketbook!" Sometimes the last one of the three is the hardest one to open.

Take Time for Joy

Leviticus 25

The New Testament abounds with joy. When Jesus was born, an angel announced "good news of great joy" (Luke 2:10). When Jesus' disciples came back after one of their preaching missions, they "returned with joy," and Jesus himself was so delighted the Bible says he was "full of joy through the Holy Spirit" (Luke 10:17, 21). The night before his crucifixion, Jesus promised his disciples that after a time of grief their "joy will be complete" (John 16:24). Joy is a fruit of the Spirit, a byproduct of God's presence in our lives (Galatians 5:22). After the Philippian jailer and his family accepted Christ, they were "filled with joy, because they had come to believe in God" (Acts 16:34). Later, the apostle Paul wrote to the Philippian church and told them, "Rejoice in the Lord always. I will say it again: Rejoice!" (Philippians 4:4).

Strangely enough, though, sometimes joy eludes us. Joy-stealers abound: discouraging events, negative people, health problems, and financial difficulties. How can we really be filled with joy in tough times like these? Part of the answer is in redefining joy. It isn't the same as happiness, which depends on our outward circumstances. Real joy is an attitude of the heart—an inner contentment, a sense of well-being that springs up inside of those who know Christ so consistently that we can "be joyful always" (John 7:37-39; 1 Thessalonians 5:16).

Even under the old covenant given through Moses, which we often stereotype as strict or even harsh, God provided a special celebration of joy for his people. It lasted for a whole year! The people called it the Year of Jubilee.

The Year of Jubilee happened every fiftieth year. This meant most people would celebrate one of these seasons of joy during their lifetime, while a fortunate few would enjoy one such year as a child and another as a senior adult.

I. WHAT JUBILEE MEANT TO THE ISRAELITES

A. Freedom from sin. "Proclaim liberty throughout the land" (v. 10). There was (at least temporarily) freedom from sin, for the Year of Jubilee began on the Day of Atonement (v. 9). On this special day, the sins of the people were symbolically transferred to the head of a goat (the "scapegoat") which was taken away into the wilderness so neither it nor the sins would return again (Leviticus 16).

B. Freedom from burdensome work. During the Year of Jubilee, the people didn't sow or reap crops from their fields. They rested and worshiped God, and he provided for their needs (vv. 11, 12).

C. Restitution of property. There were glad homecomings and reunions all over Israel, as people returned to the land originally owned by their families (v. 13). The land couldn't be sold permanently, for every 50 years it reverted to its original owner (vv. 23, 24). In fact, the selling price of real estate was determined by the number of years remaining before the Year of Jubilee (vv. 14-17).

D. Freedom from slavery. Hired workers were released from bondage during the Year of Jubilee (vv. 35-43).

II. WHAT JUBILEE MEANS TO CHRISTIANS

A. It illustrates our liberty in Christ. Jesus came to set the captives free (Isaiah 61:1; Luke 4:16-21; John 8:31-36). No matter what else is happening in our lives, we can rejoice because we're free from guilt, free from purposelessness, free from despair, free from the fear of death, free to serve the Lord (Galatians 5:1, 13; James 1:12; 1 Peter 2:16).

B. It reminds us to look forward to our future rest in Heaven. Just as the Israelites enjoyed an extended season of Sabbath rest during the Year of Jubilee, Christians joyfully look forward to our eternal home where "they will rest from their labor" (Revelation 14:13; see also Hebrews 4:9-11).

C. It reminds us a time of joyful restoration is coming when loved ones will be reunited, rights will be wronged, and justice will be done. No matter what happens to us, we can experience joy in Christ as we "look forward to the day of God and speed its coming" (2 Peter 3:12).

ILLUSTRATIONS

Say it again. Even a single command from God carries divine authority and demands our obedience. But it certainly gets our attention when the Bible repeats a command. This is the case when the apostle Paul writes, "Rejoice in the Lord always. I will say it again: Rejoice!" (Philippians 4:4). As if that were not enough, elsewhere Paul wrote, "Be joyful always" (1 Thessalonians 5:16). These verses imply: (1) To some extent at least, joy is a choice we make, an attitude we willingly adopt rather than a feeling that depends on our outward circumstances—or else the Lord couldn't command us to do it. (2) It's a difficult choice—so from time to time we need to remind one another to accept and experience the real joy that comes only from the Lord.

Can you picture them smiling? Some folks appear so serious, it's hard to imagine them with a smile on their faces. This is certainly true with many of the characters described in the Bible, for they had serious work to do, and often faced difficult hardships. Yet a great roster of Bible characters wrote about their joy in the Lord: David sang, "My heart leaps for joy" (Psalm 28:7). Solomon wrote, "A cheerful look brings joy to the heart" (Proverbs 15:30). Isaiah wrote, "With joy you will draw water from the wells of salvation" (Isaiah 12:3). There's more joy in the Bible than we often think—and plenty awaiting us in Heaven.

Bless You!

Numbers 6:22-27

We use the word *blessing* in many different ways. Some folks say "bless you" when someone sneezes. We say a "blessing" before we eat our meals. We sing "God Bless America," and hymns like "Blessed Be the Name of the Lord." Every year at Thanksgiving, we count our blessings. But what does a blessing really mean?

Patriarchs like Isaac and Jacob offered special prayers of blessing for their children (Genesis 27:27-29; 48:12-16; 49:28). Moses did the same for the Israelites (Deuteronomy 33:1-29). Jesus left his disciples with a blessing when he ascended back to Heaven (Luke 24:50-53).

The word *makarios* ("blessed") is the one Jesus repeatedly used in the Beatitudes (Matthew 5:1-12). Another term, *eulogeo*, means "to speak well of" someone or to "say a good word" (like a eulogy at a funeral). A blessing can be some good word or good gift God grants to his people (Ephesians 1:3), or it can refer to words of honor and praise we give back to God (Psalm 103:1, *King James Version*). In a sense, what was true of Abraham can be true of all of us: God blesses us, so we in turn can be a vehicle of blessing to others (Genesis 12:2, 3).

One of the most beautiful and best-known blessings in all the Bible appears in Numbers 6, where God gave the priests words of blessing to pour upon the people like a cascade of refreshing, life-giving water on parched, thirsty ground.

I. THE PRIESTLY BLESSING (NUMBERS 6:22-27)

A. The giver of blessing: the Lord.
1. Each section (vv. 24, 25, and 26) begins with "the Lord."
2. We can't manufacture true blessings; they come from the hand of God.

B. The vehicles of blessing: the priests (sons of Aaron).
1. Christ, the ultimate high priest, is the ultimate vehicle of God's blessing, the one mediator between God and man (1 Timothy 2:3-6; Hebrews 9:23-28).
2. Christians are a "royal priesthood," a "kingdom and priests" (1 Peter 2:9; Revelation 1:6). God wants us to follow the example of Jesus and be vehicles of blessing to others.

C. The receivers of blessing: "you."
1. Six times in three verses, God says to Israel that these words of blessing are for you . . . yes, you!

2. The apostle Peter offered a similar word of encouragement on the Day of Pentecost when he said, "The promise is for you and your children and for all who are far off . . ." (Acts 2:39). God's blessings of forgiveness and grace aren't simply for someone else; they're for you!

D. The dimensions of blessing. There are six specific promises contained in these short verses. The Lord will . . .
1. *Bless you:* the overall promise of God's good will.
2. *Keep you:* the reassuring promise of God's protection and watchful care.
3. *Make his face shine upon you:* the glorious promise of living in the light of God's truth (Romans 13:12; Ephesians 5:8-14; 1 Thessalonians 5:5).
4. *Be gracious to you:* the promise of God's kindness, ultimately realized in Christ Jesus (John 1:14; Ephesians 2:8-10).
5. *Turn his face toward you:* the promise of a positive, personal relationship with the Creator, ultimately realized in Heaven (Revelation 22:4).
6. *Give you peace:* the promise of what the Hebrews called *shalom,* an all-encompassing well-being only God can give (see John 14:27; Romans 5:1).

II. THE LIFE OF BLESSING WE CAN LIVE

A. We need to receive God's blessings ourselves, especially the greatest one of all: eternal life in Christ.

B. We need to extend God's blessings to others through our families, our neighborhoods, and our world.

ILLUSTRATIONS

Sins forgotten. Friedrich Nietzsche once wrote, "Blessed are the forgetful, for they get the better even of their blunders." But the psalmist David pointed out a far better blessing: "Blessed is he whose transgressions are forgiven, whose sins are covered. Blessed is the man whose sin the LORD does not count against him and in whose spirit is no deceit" (Psalm 32:1, 2).

Face lift. When Jesus first encountered two discouraged disciples on the road to Emmaus, their faces were downcast (Luke 24:17). But after Jesus spent time with them and opened their minds to the Scripture, their eyes were open and their vision clear (Luke 24:30-32). When the Lord turns his face toward us in blessing (Numbers 6:26), it gives us a lift like nothing else.

Voices of Faith, Voices of Doubt

Numbers 13 & 14

Faith can move mountains, according to Jesus. But we want to know, "Can it move *my* mountain?" Even a tiny amount of faith, the size of a mustard seed, can grow into something enormous and productive. But how should we respond when doubts threaten to extinguish the seed of faith? How can we hear God's "still, small voice" when the voices of doubt shout so loudly and persistently?

As Moses led the Israelites toward the promised land, the time came to scout out the land. The Lord told Moses to select and send one leader from each of Israel's 12 tribes (13:1-16). Some strategic military decisions needed to be made before the Israelites could begin their invasion, so Moses instructed the 12 spies to conduct a thorough investigation of the land, its people, the fertility and fruitfulness of the soil, and the strength of the cities' fortifications (13:17-20).

The spies' dangerous mission lasted 40 days. When they returned carrying an impressive array of grapes, pomegranates, and figs, a large assembly of people gathered to hear their report (13:21-26). There was plenty of good news to tell: the land indeed flowed "with milk and honey" as God had promised (13:27). But in the face of danger, it's often easier to respond with fear instead of faith.

I. VOICES OF DOUBT

A. The spies' majority opinion? The land of Canaan is wonderful but unwinnable. They saw the problems more than they saw the prospects. They mainly saw obstacles, not opportunities.

B. No doubt some of the skeptical spies' concerns were legitimate. The Canaanites and their cities were indeed large, powerful, and intimidating (13:28). The "descendants of Anak" loomed overhead like giants (13:31-33). But while the potential hardships meant the task would be difficult, they didn't mean that the task would be impossible!

C. The doubtful spies illustrate several problems with fear:
1. Fear magnifies small problems into insurmountable ones. Faithlessness transforms spiritual molehills into unclimbable mountains. Some of the spies' descriptions sound like they were exaggerated by fear. "The land we explored devours those living in it" (13:32). Really? Then how did the spies themselves survive 40 days there? "All the people we saw there are of great size" (13:32). Really? *All* of them?

2. Fear leads to unrealistic and negative thoughts about ourselves and what we can accomplish. "We seemed like grasshoppers in our own eyes" (13:33).

3. Fear is contagious! Because 10 spies highlighted their fears, soon "all the people of the community raised their voices and wept aloud" (14:1). Soon a widespread attitude of negativity and rebellion pervaded the camp (14:2-4, 36, 37).

II. VOICES OF FAITH

A. The spies' minority report? "We can do this!" Two of the 12 spies, Joshua and Caleb, spoke a positive message of faith: "We should go up . . . we can certainly do it" (13:30). The land "is exceedingly good" (14:7). The Lord "will lead us into that land . . . and will give it to us" (14:8). "Do not be afraid" (14:9).

B. The most important factor, completely omitted by the clamoring voices of doubt, appears in 14:9: "the Lord is with us."

C. Faith *doesn't* mean: putting our heads in the sand . . . overlooking real problems . . . ignoring legitimate criticism and concerns . . . stifling discussion and problem-solving . . . acting with foolish or reckless abandon.

D. Faith *does* mean: taking a stand for what's right, even when the majority doesn't agree . . . resisting negative and pessimistic attitudes . . . daring to speak out and challenge the status quo . . . being willing to take a risk once you're sure it's a risk God endorses . . . trusting in God's wisdom and power instead of your own.

E. In the final analysis, what determines our destiny will not be the voices of others but the choices we ourselves make. Will we decide to listen to the voices of doubt, or the voices of faith? One of those two faithful spies later said it very well: "Choose for yourselves this day whom you will serve. . . . But as for me and my household, we will serve the Lord" (Joshua 24:15).

ILLUSTRATIONS

Dare mighty things. In a speech delivered before the Hamilton Club in Chicago, April 10, 1899, Theodore Roosevelt said, "Far better it is to dare mighty things, to win glorious triumphs, even though checkered by failure, than to take rank with those poor spirits who neither enjoy much nor suffer much, because they live in the gray twilight that knows not victory nor defeat."

Dare to do the unthinkable. Major league baseball's single season home run record stood at 61 for 37 years until 1998, when not one man but two surpassed it (Mark McGwire hit 70, Sammy Sosa hit 66). Great achievements are possible with God's help, but we must dare to dream, step out, and obey.

Love Rules

Deuteronomy 6:5;
Leviticus 19:18

Love, someone has said, is "the oxygen of God's kingdom." "Knowledge puffs up, but love builds up," the apostle Paul wrote (1 Corinthians 8:1). Few words from the lips of Jesus cut much deeper than his sad warning in John 5:42, "I know that you do not have the love of God in your hearts."

Even though all of God's laws are important, it's not surprising that the Lord Jesus identified two rules of love from the Law of Moses as the "greatest commandments in the Law." When we follow these two "love rules," they will bind together all the other Christian virtues and allow the peace of Christ to "rule in your hearts" (Colossians 3:14, 15).

I. LOVE GOD WITH YOUR WHOLE SELF (DEUTERONOMY 6:5).

A. Our love for God is *volitional* (an act of the will). This verse is a positive command to obey, something we must choose to do.

B. Our love for him must be *personal*. "Love the Lord your God." (Have you claimed him as your own Lord and Savior?)

C. Our love for God must be *practical*—a love that flows out of every aspect of what we think and say and do. "Love God," Moses wrote, "with all your heart and with all your soul and with all your strength." (Incidentally, in Matthew 22:37 Jesus added "and with all your mind," underscoring the importance of growing in our understanding of God and his will.) Love for God is something we live, not just something we feel. In practical terms, love for God means:
  1. Reverence—approaching God with profound respect and awe when we worship him (Hebrews 12:28, 29).
  2. Gratitude—maintaining a deep, constant appreciation for God's blessings (Colossians 3:17; 1 Thessalonians 5:18).
  3. Humility—remembering that "God is in heaven and [we] are on earth" (Ecclesiastes 5:2), we "humble [ourselves] . . . under God's mighty hand," knowing that in due time he will lift us up (1 Peter 5:6).
  4. Trust—remaining confident that God is always working for our good and knows what is best for us (Romans 8:28).
  5. Obedience—staying ready to do whatever God asks (1 John 5:3; 2 John 6).
  6. Commitment—choosing to be faithful until death (Revelation 2:10).

7. Discernment—learning to love what God loves, and hate what God hates (Psalm 97:10; 101:3; Proverbs 6:16-19).
8. Friendship—developing a bond of affection that moves us to serve God not merely out of obligation but out of joyful desire (John 15:9-15).

II. LOVE YOUR NEIGHBOR AS YOURSELF (LEVITICUS 19:18).
A. Do you want to live like a king? Then follow "the royal law" (James 2:8).

B. Love for our neighbors does *not* mean:
1. Approving of sin in a person's life. We can hate sin, but love the sinner, as Jesus did (John 8:11).
2. Feeling the same sentiment toward all people. Even Jesus had a special friendship with Mary, Martha, Lazarus, and his disciple John (John 11:5; 13:23).
3. Having no special obligations toward those closest to us. We have especially keen obligations to care for other Christians (Galatians 6:10), and for our closest neighbors of all—members of our immediate families (Ephesians 5:33; 1 Timothy 5:8).

C. Love for our neighbors *does* mean:
1. Recognizing the value of every person, regardless of wealth, race, or social class (James 2:1-9).
2. Making every person the object of our goodwill. Jesus' classic illustration of neighbor love is the story of the Good Samaritan who cared enough to serve a wounded man who needed his help (Luke 10:25-37).
3. Being unselfish and generous in our dealings with others, especially those whom others tend to overlook (Luke 14:12-14; Romans 13:7-10; 1 John 3:16).
4. Being willing to forgive (Matthew 18:21-35; Luke 17:3-5).
5. Refraining from a hypercritical, judgmental attitude toward others (Matthew 7:1-5; Romans 12:17-21).
6. Growing toward maturity by following the pattern for love outlined in 1 Corinthians 13.

ILLUSTRATIONS
Growing in love. I was married on August 31, 1975. Knowing that God calls husbands to love our wives as Christ loved the church (Ephesians 5:25), and recognizing that my own ability to love was imperfect and immature, I determined that I would read 1 Corinthians 13 once each day during the entire month of August leading up to my wedding day. I read it 31 times—and I've read it many more times in the quarter of a century since. I still have a long way to go (just ask my wife!), but I'm thankful that God not only tells us we ought to love; he gives us a clear description of the way we're to act as we grow in love.

Undying love. Ephesians 6:24 says, "Grace to all who love our Lord Jesus Christ with an undying love." His love led him to die for us. Our love for him must never die.

Never Forget

Deuteronomy 8:6-20

Forgetting can get us into trouble. (Did you ever forget to pay a bill, water a plant, return a phone call, or attend a meeting?) It can cause embarrassment. (Did you ever forget a person's name, or forget to do something you promised to do?) Worse, it can cause us spiritual harm.

Second Peter 1:9 warns that it's possible for a person to become spiritually nearsighted and blind and forget "that he has been cleansed from his past sins." When they were on the verge of entering the promised land, Moses gave the people of Israel some urgent warnings about important truths they (and we) should never forget.

I. BE GRATEFUL . . .

A. For spiritual blessings (v. 6).
1. How thankful we should be for God's revealed Word that makes known his commands, his ways, and his holy character.
2. Even more, how thankful we should be for our salvation purchased by the blood of Christ, and the Holy Spirit who indwells us!

B. For physical blessings (vv. 7-10).
1. Do you live in a "good land"? Have you found that your bread is not "scarce," and that God has consistently met your needs? Thank him!
2. "When you have eaten and are satisfied, praise the Lord your God" (v. 10). We shouldn't just thank God for our food before we eat it, but afterward too!

II. BE CAREFUL . . .

A. That you don't forget God (vv. 11-14).
1. Material comforts can lead to spiritual apathy.
2. Present ease can make us forget past struggles.

B. That you don't become prideful (vv. 15-18).
1. We aren't good enough to deserve the kindness God is willing to give.
2. We aren't strong enough to produce the blessings only God can give.

III. BE MINDFUL . . .

A. Of spiritual danger (v. 19).

1. Satan is a tempter (Matthew 4:1), a deceiver (John 8:44), a devourer (1 Peter 5:8), a masquerader (2 Corinthians 11:14), and a destroyer (Revelation 9:11).
2. One of the devil's chief strategies is to confront us continually with appealing alternatives (idols) that compete for the place only God should occupy. We need to recognize the devil's tactics and resist him firmly (James 4:7).

B. Of God's judgment (v. 20).
1. All of us are accountable to God (Romans 14:12; 2 Corinthians 5:10).
2. It changes our entire perspective when we conduct our lives in the constant awareness of our coming appointment before the throne of God.
3. If we never forget what God has done in the past, and we never forget what God will do in the future, we will know what to do in the present!

ILLUSTRATIONS

Thankful hearts. When the apostle Paul described the terrible times coming in the last days, he not only wrote that people will be abusive, unforgiving, and brutal; he also included "ungrateful" as one of the marks of ever-increasing sin (2 Timothy 3:1-4). Ingratitude is a serious evil—a sign that we have forgotten our Creator (Romans 1:21). But a truly thankful heart gives honor to the Lord and draws others to him. That's why Paul also wrote that Christians should always be in the habit of "giving thanks to God the Father" through Christ (Colossians 3:17).

Don't forget to eat. Most of us have no problem remembering to eat our meals. But we dare not forget to partake of the spiritual food Christ offers to nourish our souls (John 6:53-58). Perhaps that is why the Lord instituted the Lord's Supper and said, "Do this in remembrance of me" (1 Corinthians 11:23-25). We are forgetful people, but as often as we partake of it, the Lord's Supper reminds us what it cost for us to be saved.

What Makes Life Worthwhile?

Psalm 90

What makes life worthwhile? Solomon tried to find out, and he concluded that the main point of life is to "fear God and keep his commandments" (Ecclesiastes 12:13). Jesus said that we "save" our lives only when we "lose" them (Mark 8:35). The apostle Paul summarized his life's purpose as a quest to "know Christ and the power of his resurrection" and to share in "the fellowship of sharing in his sufferings" (Philippians 3:10).

Moses reached a similar conclusion, which he expressed in a beautiful prayer in Psalm 90 (the only prayer of Moses recorded in the book of Psalms). This psalm challenges us to rearrange our priorities and make the best possible use of our time so that our lives will count to the utmost in service to the Lord.

I. OUR EVERLASTING GOD (vv. 1-4)

A. He is Lord over all generations (v. 1). Whether we're young, old, or somewhere in between, as the years pass by it makes sense to hang on to the one who is "the same yesterday and today and forever" (Hebrews 13:8).

B. He is Lord over life and death (vv. 2, 3). He is the Alpha and the Omega, the Beginning and the End, the First and the Last. This applies to all of creation (for God created all things and will bring all things to an end when the time is right). It also applies to each of us individually (for God gave us life, and he alone can give us hope of eternal life when we die).

C. He is Lord over time (v. 4). God sees time from an eternal perspective. He can cram a millennium's worth of meaning into a single day (like the day Jesus died on the cross) and he can wait patiently while a millennium passes if it suits his timetable to wait (see 2 Peter 3:8, 9).

II. OUR FAST-MOVING DAYS (vv. 5-11)

A. Our lives pass quickly (vv. 5, 6, 10). Time flies, especially as we grow older. How quickly a big day (a wedding, a graduation, or a holiday celebration) can come and go. In the big picture of life, how quickly we move through the seasons of childhood and adulthood, like grass that turns green in the morning and turns brown in the afternoon sun. Like a vapor or a morning fog, our lives pass quickly (James 4:14). Let's not waste the time we have.

B. Our sins make our lives more burdensome (vv. 7-9, 11). Our sins not only grieve and anger the Lord; they complicate our lives as well. Guilt is like a ball and chain we drag around. When we disobey the Lord and pursue priorities other than his kingdom and his righteousness, our lives become less fulfilling.

III. THREE KEYS TO MAKE THE MOST OF OUR DAYS (vv. 12-17)

A. Management of time (v. 12). How can we "number our days"? By planning carefully and ordering our lives so that God's priorities come first. For example, does your schedule this week give priority to the Great Commandments (loving God and loving your neighbor)? Is there room in your annual calendar for Great Commission work as you "go and make disciples"? Indeed, good time management requires "a heart of wisdom." Let's ask God to provide it (James 1:5).

B. Forgiveness of sin (vv. 13-16). A worthwhile life is a forgiven, grace-filled life. The only way to make our lives count to the maximum is to seek God's mercy and compassion, freely given through Jesus Christ. Is this the year—or the day—for you to find forgiveness in Christ and give your life to him?

C. Meaningful work (v. 17). Once we've established godly priorities, we can find new satisfaction in our daily tasks. As we serve the Lord, we can pray sincerely, "Establish the work of our hands," because we know that ultimately it is God's work anyway.

ILLUSTRATIONS

Going in circles. When our family had a hamster for a pet, I noticed that its main activities were simply eating, sleeping, and running around in a little wheel we kept in its cage. What a life! When I die, I don't want my tombstone to read, "David Faust—He Ate, He Slept, He Went Around in Circles." I want my life to count for something more worthwhile than that. Don't you?

Antique collecting. When my grandfather decided to sell some of his belongings at an auction, the auctioneer was pleased. "This should be a good sale, Mr. Faust," the auctioneer said, "because you have so many antiques." "Antiques?" Grandpa immediately replied. "I don't have any antiques. Why, I never bought an antique in my life!" Sometimes life passes by so quickly we don't even realize that we, and the things we own, are aging.

I've Got a Secret

Deuteronomy 29:29

Years ago a TV show called "I've Got a Secret" featured guests who had done something notable or unusual, and by asking questions, a group of panelists tried to figure out the guests' "secrets." Some secrets are fun (a whispered promise from a smiling grandparent to an excited grandchild). Others are deadly serious (military secrets affecting national security).

But what would it be like if the truth about God and eternal life were completely secret? In one helpful verse of Scripture (Deuteronomy 29:29), Moses gave us powerful words that explain some of the mysteries of life and godliness.

I. SOME THINGS ONLY GOD KNOWS FOR SURE. "THE SECRET THINGS BELONG TO THE LORD OUR GOD" (v. 29a).

A. "Secret things." How marvelous is the vast wisdom and knowledge of God! We don't know how many hairs are on our heads; but he knows. We don't comprehend all the mysteries of life or how a baby is knit together in his mother's womb (Psalm 139:13); but God knows. We ask, "Why do the innocent suffer? Why do we face so many problems here on earth? What about Bible passages that are hard to understand?" It's normal—even healthy—to ask questions, for they can help us grow in our faith and wisdom. But there will always be "secret things" only God comprehends.

B. "Belong to God." Many of life's mysteries we can figure out. Those that we can't figure out are not our property anyway; they are God's. We shouldn't try to take what doesn't belong to us. Ultimately the church isn't ours, but the Lord's (Matthew 16:18). Our bodies don't belong to us, but to him (1 Corinthians 6:19, 20). Likewise, we need to humbly recognize God's lordship over our intellectual curiosity. Search for understanding, but accept the fact that ultimate answers belong to the Lord. That's what Job finally realized (Job 42:1-6).

II. SOME THINGS WE KNOW FOR SURE. THANK THE LORD, NOT EVERYTHING IS A SECRET! "THE THINGS REVEALED BELONG TO US AND TO OUR CHILDREN FOREVER" (v. 29b).

A. "Things revealed." God has let us in on many of his "secrets"! Some of the most important issues we wonder about aren't secrets anymore. Questions previous generations wondered about have been cleared up with the coming of Christ (Matthew 13:16, 17; 1 Peter 1:10-12). Does God exist? Does he love us? Do our lives have any significance? What is right, and what is wrong? How can we be saved from our sins and live forever after we die? All of these questions and hundreds more, God has answered openly—in writing in the Bible, and in person through his Son Jesus Christ (Hebrews 1:1-3; Romans 1:18-20; 1 Corinthians 2:10; Galatians 1:12; Ephesians 3:2-5; 1 Timothy 3:16).

B. "Belong to us and to our children forever."
1. We need to "own" these truths—embrace them so they truly "belong to us."
2. We need to pass these truths along to the next generation so God's will won't be a secret to them (Deuteronomy 6:4-9; Ephesians 6:4; 2 Timothy 2:2).
3. We need to respect the permanence of God's revealed truths (they belong to us "forever"). In every culture and every age, Christ and his Word abide (Hebrews 13:8; Jude 3; Revelation 22:18, 19).

III. THE THINGS WE *KNOW* SHOW US THINGS TO *DO.* "THAT WE MAY FOLLOW ALL THE WORDS OF THIS LAW" (v. 29c).

A. By itself, knowledge of God's truth isn't enough. We need to translate it into action. It's not enough to quote the Golden Rule if we mistreat our neighbors and families. It's not enough to recite the Lord's Prayer if we really aren't interested in the Father's will being done and his kingdom expanding. "If you love me, you will obey what I command" (John 14:15).

B. Instead of worrying about what we *don't* know about God, we need to obey and put into practice what we *do* know. God has revealed enough to keep us busy for a lifetime. And that's no secret!

ILLUSTRATIONS

Open the curtain. Did you ever attend a play or a concert at a theater? Think of the excitement that fills the audience shortly before the curtain opens. Finally the moment arrives and the curtain opens, allowing us to see for ourselves what is onstage. By revealing himself to mankind, God has "opened the curtain" and given us clear, wonderful glimpses of his truth. But there's more. Even after the theater curtain opens there are things going on backstage that we don't see. Unseen, the producer, director, and stage crew work behind the scenes. Yes, God has "opened the curtain" to us and revealed his work. But we need to trust him to handle the things going on "backstage."

Information overload. Our culture is saturated with information via the Internet, TV, radio, newspapers, magazines, books, billboards—even church bulletins and newsletters. If that isn't enough, plenty of people around us are willing to let us know what they think and what we should do! Yet with all the voices clamoring for our attention, one Voice stands out. Do we listen to the voice of God as he speaks to us through his Word?

The Death of a Godly Man

Deuteronomy 34:1-12

The Bible says, "Precious in the sight of the LORD is the death of his saints" (Psalm 116:15). These words are comforting, but puzzling too. What is precious about the death of a man or woman who has served God? It's especially hard to see anything precious about death when we're feeling keenly the loss of a person who was precious to us. Deuteronomy chapter 34 tells about the death of Moses. What was precious about the death of Moses?

I. GOD BLESSED HIM IN LIFE.

A. Before Moses died, God gave him a glimpse of what his life's work had meant. He "climbed Mount Nebo," from which he could enjoy a panoramic view of the promised land (vv. 1-4). Although Moses himself wasn't allowed to enter the land because of his previous disobedience (Numbers 20:1-13), God graciously allowed him to see the beauties of Canaan.

B. Every person's lifetime on earth matters in the overall plan of God. When you and I reach the end of our lives, will we see the part our lives played in God's purposes? Moses lived long enough to recognize the fulfillment of God's promises made centuries before to Abraham, Isaac, and Jacob (v. 4).

II. GOD WAS WITH HIM IN DEATH.

A. Isn't it interesting that when Moses died, this man of God received such a simple epitaph? "Moses the servant of the Lord died" (v. 5). He had accomplished unprecedented achievements, but it was enough to simply say he was a "servant of the Lord." When you and I die, won't that be enough for us too?

B. There's a tender beauty, and a subtle irony, about Moses' funeral arrangements. God himself performed the burial without fanfare or a big crowd in attendance. How strange that this man who had such an impact upon history was buried in a private ceremony, and no one knows the location of his grave except God (v. 6)! According to Jude 9, the devil tried to lay some sort of claim on the body of Moses (perhaps so later generations of believers would be tempted to turn Moses' tomb into a shrine). But in his wisdom, God buried Moses in private. No one else may know the location of Moses' body, but God knows where Moses is. In eternity, Moses is still alive and serving his Lord (Matthew 17:1-5).

C. Jesus received a tender, private burial as well, at the hands of his friends Nicodemus and Joseph of Arimathea. But because he later rose from the dead, we can have assurance that we will be in the presence of the Lord ourselves after we die (1 Corinthians 15:1-3, 55-58; Philippians 1:21-24).

III. GOD'S PEOPLE GRIEVED FOR HIM — BUT NOT FOREVER.

A. Moses died at the ripe old age of 120, "yet his eyes were not weak nor his strength gone" (v. 7). God continued to use Moses powerfully right up to the time of his death. In fact, his last 40 years were his most significant years of service.

B. Recognizing the gravity of their loss, the people of Israel grieved for Moses. Even though we have the hope of eternal life, we experience deep sadness when a loved one dies. But the mourning need not continue forever. The Israelites grieved for Moses for one month, and then "the time of weeping and mourning was over" (v. 8). Christians grieve, but not "like the rest of men, who have no hope" (1 Thessalonians 4:13). We look forward to a reunion in that place where all death and mourning and weeping and pain will be gone forever (Revelation 21:4).

IV. GOD'S WORK WENT ON.

A. Even someone as great as Moses wasn't indispensable. God's work must go on in every generation, so the Lord had prepared a capable younger man to be Moses' successor. Moses willingly participated in this passing of the baton. Before he died, he "laid his hands" on Joshua and imparted a special gift of wisdom to this one who would carry on God's work (v. 9).

B. Moses died in victory, leaving behind an impressive legacy of service (vv. 10-12). What will people say about us when we die? And more importantly, have we accepted God's saving grace in Christ so that we will be ready to face death with assurance and hope?

ILLUSTRATIONS

Funeral arrangements. Someone pointed out that Jesus disrupted every funeral he ever attended by raising the deceased from the dead! It's hard to imagine, though, that Jairus the synagogue ruler (Mark 5), the widow at Nain (Luke 7), or Mary and Martha (John 11) considered Jesus' intervention unwelcome! The most important "funeral arrangements" are the ones we make long before we die—by accepting Christ as Savior and Lord, and allowing him to remove death's "sting" (1 Corinthians 15:56).

Life sentences. Enoch's epitaph? "He walked with God" (Genesis 5:24). A king named Omri? "He did evil in the eyes of the LORD and sinned more than all those before him" (1 Kings 16:25). Mary of Bethany? "She did what she could" (Mark 14:8). If someone were to summarize your life in one sentence, what would that person say?